Anonymous

The Centenary Commemoration of the Birth of Dr. William Ellery Channing, April 7th, 1880

Reports of the meetings in London, Belfast, Aberdeen, Tavistock, Manchester and Liverpool

Anonymous

The Centenary Commemoration of the Birth of Dr. William Ellery Channing, April 7th, 1880
Reports of the meetings in London, Belfast, Aberdeen, Tavistock, Manchester and Liverpool

ISBN/EAN: 9783337092535

Printed in Europe, USA, Canada, Australia, Japan

Cover: Foto ©ninafisch / pixelio.de

More available books at **www.hansebooks.com**

THE

CENTENARY COMMEMORATION

OF THE BIRTH OF

DR. WILLIAM ELLERY CHANNING

APRIL 7th, 1880.

REPORTS OF THE MEETINGS

IN LONDON, BELFAST, ABERDEEN, TAVISTOCK, MANCHESTER, AND LIVERPOOL.

LONDON.
BRITISH & FOREIGN UNITARIAN ASSOCIATION
37, NORFOLK STREET, STRAND.

1880.

The British and Foreign Unitarian Association, in accordance with its First Rule, gives publicity to works calculated "to promote Unitarian Christianity by the diffusion of Biblical, theological, and literary knowledge, on topics connected with it," but does not hold itself responsible for every statement, opinion or expression of the writers.

NOTICE.

It had been intended to publish the Report of the Commemoration in London separately, but at the meeting of the Council of the British and Foreign Unitarian Association, April 21st, the resolution was adopted to extend the plan of publication so as to include reports of similar meetings in Belfast, Manchester, Liverpool, and elsewhere.

The arrangement of the reports in this volume follows the order of time in which the meetings were held, and it was considered that, although some delay in the publication would necessarily be involved, the book would gain in permanent value if the principal Addresses were revised, as they have been, by the speakers themselves.

The Reports of the Meetings which were held in America at Newport, Brooklyn, Boston, Cincinnati, and Chicago, are also expected to appear in a combined form. It was announced at the laying of the cornerstone of the Memorial Church at Newport, that the $50,000 required for the building had been subscribed for.

CONTENTS.

	PAGE
THE MEETING IN ST. JAMES'S HALL, LONDON	5
THE MEETING IN THE MUSIC HALL, BELFAST	98
THE MEETING IN BLACKFRIARS STREET HALL, ABERDEEN	119
THE MEETING IN THE GUILDHALL, TAVISTOCK	127
THE MEETING IN THE TOWN HALL, MANCHESTER	131
THE MEETING IN ST. GEORGE'S HALL, LIVERPOOL	175
ARTICLES AND NOTICES—	
FROM THE CHRISTIAN WORLD	219
FROM THE PALL MALL GAZETTE	225
FROM THE DAILY TELEGRAPH	231
FROM THE DAILY NEWS	238
FROM THE ANTI-SLAVERY REPORTER	243
FROM THE METHODIST	244
FROM THE CHRISTIAN GLOBE	245
FROM THE INQUIRER	249
FROM THE UNITARIAN HERALD	251
FROM THE CHRISTIAN LIFE	253

THE CHANNING CENTENARY COMMEMORATION,

St. JAMES'S HALL, LONDON.

AT the meeting of the Council of the British and Foreign Unitarian Association, in the beginning of the present year, the Executive Committee were requested to take measures for celebrating, on the 7th of April, the Centenary of the birth of Dr. William Ellery Channing. In accordance with this instruction, it was resolved to hold on that day a Soirée and Public Meeting, with the view of inviting public attention to the various aspects of Dr. Channing's work and influence as a Christian teacher, the opponent of slavery and war, the advocate of temperance and popular education, and of every cause tending to promote the liberty and elevation of mankind. The appeal made upon this broad ground was for the most part well responded to by ministers and laymen of various religious denominations, and especially by the representatives of different forms of philanthropic work in the metropolis. How deep and how widely spread was the desire to honour the memory of Dr. Channing was shown by the assembling of a large and sympathetic audience, notwithstanding that many influential friends, members of Parliament and others, were unable to attend on account of the sudden calls of political duty at the time.

Amongst those whose absence was due to this special cause were several gentlemen, who would otherwise have taken part in the meeting—Mr. William Rathbone, the member for Liverpool in the late Parliament, Mr. J. W. Probyn, and Mr. Henry Richard, the member for Merthyr Tydfil, who has publicly expressed his profound appreciation of Dr. Channing's character and writings.

Many letters were received from others, also regretting their inability to be present, besides those to whom reference was specifically made during the meeting; for example, from Sir James C. Lawrence, M.P., Miss F. Power Cobbe, Dr. G. Vance Smith, Rev. John Hunter, of York, Rev. J. T. Stannard, of Huddersfield, Miss Davenport Hill, Mr. H. Spicer, Lord Arthur Russell, Rev. J. A. Picton, Rev. E. R. Ground, Rev. J. Saunders, Mr. James Heywood, F.R.S., and Mr. J. Fretwell, Rev. R. Tuck, Rev. J. Macnaught, Rev. W. Young, Rev. Johnson Barker, Rev. H. Griffith, Rev. Dr. A. J. Ross, Rev. Dr. Bailey, and others, many of whom gratefully acknowledged their obligations to Dr. Channing, and their reverence for his memory. The letter of the gentleman last named offers a fair example of the replies to the invitations of the Committee. Dr. Bailey wrote:

" Had I been in town I should have rejoiced to be present, as a mark of my profound esteem for one who, by his goodness, his genius, and his devotion to freedom and progress, as well as by his magnificent writings, is an honour to the human race." The feeling expressed by the Rev. H. Griffith, in a few striking words, is evidently shared by a large number of persons—" The memory of Dr. Channing is to me a very sacred treasure."

The Meeting was held in St. James's Hall, which was filled in almost every part. Near the organ were draped the flags of the United States and of Great Britain, and the platform and orchestra were decorated with evergreens and flowers—an expression of sympathy with the commemoration on the part of a lady, who, nevertheless, preferred that her kind contribution to the success of the occasion should be an anonymous one.

Tea having been served to a constant succession of parties in a large room adjoining the Great Hall, an appropriate selection of music from Handel, Mendelssohn, and others, was admirably played on the fine organ by Mr. Thomas Pettit, A.R.A.M., the organist of the Bach Choir, most agreeably occupying the hour until the period fixed for the Public Meeting, for which a large number of free tickets had been issued. Of those who were present, either on the platform or in the body of the meeting, besides the gentlemen who took part in the proceedings, were observed Mrs. Edwin Arnold and her son; the Revs. D. Amos; Dr. Aveling; C. M. Birrell;

Prof. J. E. Carpenter, M.A.; G. Carter; J. Charlesworth; P. W. Clayden; C. Corkran; T. Crow; Dr. S. Davidson; Valentine Davis; T. Dobson (Brighton); Prof. James Drummond, B.A.; R. B. Drummond, B.A. (Edinburgh); J. G. Evans (Preston); T. W. Freckelton; J. S. Forsyth; M. C. Gascoigne; E. M. Geldart, M.A.; J. P. Ham; J. T. Heard (Caterham); P. M. Higginson, M.A. (Styal); J. N. Hoare; C. Howe; R. C. Jones; T. F. Lockyer, B.A.; J. R. M'Kee; T. L. Marshall; J. Martin; W. J. Odgers; C. W. Oxford; W. Pankridge; Prof. E. H. Plumptre; C. Rae; T. Rix; Dr. Sadler; C. Shakspeare; J. Shannon; J. D. H. Smyth; H. Solly; R. Spears; John Stanton; J. E. Stead; F. Storrs Turner, B.A. (Secretary of the Anti-Opium Society); F. Summers; J. Taylor; Prof. C. B. Upton; W. Urwick; J. T. Whitehead; C. Wicksteed, B.A.; P. H. Wicksteed, M.A.; Mark Wilks; Jeffery Worthington; Dr. Wysard (German Lutheran Church); C. H. Allen (Secretary of the Anti-Slavery Society); Dr. L. M. Aspland; T. Barrow; R. Bartram; E. Bromley; F. W. Chesson (Aborigines Protection Society); James Clarke, jun.; T. Chatfeild Clarke; E. Clodd; T. P. Cobb; A. Collier; F. Collier; M. D. Conway, M.A.; W. Coupland; P. N. Dattar; C. J. G. Eiloart; R. Eve (Aldershot); A. J. C. Fabritius; T. Gregory Foster; R. Glover, J.P.; W. P. Greenway; J. T. Hart; Dr. Haward; A. Higginson, J. Hobson; W. Hudson; H. Jeffery; Courtney S. Kenny (Downing College, Cambridge); G. Lawford; E. Lawrence, LL.B; T. S. Lister; Dr. Longstaff; Meadows Martineau, J.P.; C. P. Mason (Fellow of University

College, London); C. E. Mudie; F. Nettlefold; R. S. Oakshott; J. D. Parley; J. Philp; E. Plimpton; J. T. Preston; S. W. Preston; Robert Rae; T. Reed; W. Shaen, M.A.; W. A. Sharpe; T. Smith Osler, Q.C.; W. Spiller; Howard Miss Anna Swanwick; W. Tallack (Secretary of the Society); N. M. Tayler; S. S. Tayler; W. Titford; J. Troup; Denis Varga; I. M. Wade; C. Watson; J. Carvell Williams (Liberation Society); Dr. Wylde, etc., etc.

THE PUBLIC MEETING.

DAVID MARTINEAU, ESQ., the President of the Association, having taken the chair, the following hymn, by J. Mason Neale, was sung (to the tune 'Weber') with much spirit and feeling by the whole assembly.

> They whose course on earth is o'er,
> Think they of their brethren more?
> They before the throne who bow,
> Feel they for their brethren now?
>
> Yea, the holy dead have still
> Part in all our joy and ill;
> One in heart, and one in love;
> We below, and they above.

Those whom many a land divides,
Many mountains, many tides,
Have they with each other part?
Have they fellowship in heart?

Each to each may be unknown,
Wide apart their lots be thrown;
Differing tongues their lips may speak;
One be strong, and one be weak:

Yet in tear, and sigh, and prayer,
Each with other hath a share;
With each other join they here
In affliction, doubt, and fear.

So with them our hearts we raise,
Share their work, and join their praise;
Blessed pledge that we shall be
Joined, O Lord, in bliss with Thee.

The REV. PROFESSOR DRUMMOND offered the prayer—
"O God, the Father of all spirits, in whom those who love thee in heaven and on earth are united in one great family, we thank thee for all thy saints who have borne a faithful witness to divine things, and left behind them a blessed memory to dwell as a sanctifying power in our hearts, and lift our affections towards the eternal world. We thank thee for him whose name we hold in such sacred remembrance this night, and would glorify thee for having put thy Spirit upon him, and through his words and through his life drawn so many souls to thy-

self. Grant, O Father, that we may take home with greater impressiveness to our hearts the lofty wisdom, the world-wide justice, the large and mighty love towards thee and towards all thy children, to which his life was so devoutly consecrated, that so, amidst our many and imperfect thoughts, we may feel the unity of the Spirit drawing us to one another, and that we too may be humbly instrumental in making the glorious Gospel of thy Son a living and exalting power in society, and may help on that better time when every proud and jealous passion shall be subdued into thy peace, and when the gracious truths proclaimed by Christ shall come with soul-subduing energy to every child of man, and all churches and nations shall be baptized with the Holy Spirit, and with the fire of self-sacrificing love. With our minds filled with precious memories and brightened with undying hopes, we would toil and pray for the coming of thy kingdom, believing that thy word which has spoken in Christ, and in so many Christ-like men and women, and which is still so near to the humble and trustful soul, will never return unto thee void, but will at last accomplish thy blessed will, and make this world a forecourt of eternal life. And to thee for thy unspeakable gifts be thanksgiving and praise for ever. Amen."

The CHAIRMAN :—I would now call upon the Secretary to read some portions of the numerous letters from persons whose hearts are very cordially with us, but who have been prevented in consequence of other events taking place just now from being present this evening. I may mention that Mr. James Russell Lowell, the United States Minister at the Court of St. James's, expressed to our Secretary his deep regret that, owing to the unfortunate illness of his wife, he has been obliged to return to Madrid; otherwise he had hoped to be present. He was the author of the very beautiful elegy on Channing which was given at length in one of our papers last week.

The SECRETARY:—The Rev. Stopford A. Brooke regrets to be obliged to say that he will not be able to be in town for this meeting. He adds, "I should have liked to have acknowledged in some way my great obligations to Dr. Channing; obligations which I shall never forget, and which I can scarcely overestimate."—Dr. George Macdonald writes, "I thank you very heartily for the honour you do me in desiring my presence at your commemoration. It would have given me much pleasure to be there, but I shall not be in England so early in the year. I hope you will have somebody from Boston with you. There Channing's spirit seems to hang brooding over the place."—The Rev. George M. Murphy, of the Borough Road Congregational Church, who is so well known in connection with mission work in Lambeth, writes that he has engagements out of town to-day; otherwise "it would have given me very great pleasure to have been present to do honour to the memory of so noble a social reformer and friend of humanity."—The eminent present lecturer of the Hibbert Trust, M. Renan, says, while sincerely regretting that an engagement which he had accepted some time since for this evening will not permit him to join the Association in celebrating the centenary of the birth of Channing,— "Channing was a true prophet. He heard with a rare justice the first sounds of the bell of the future Gospel. You have reason to honour as pillars of the eternal Christianism these saints of the nineteenth century—the greatest of all—that Rome will not canonize. The doctrine of Channing, entirely a doctrine of peace and love, will remain true, whatever be the evolutions of science and of the free spirit."—Mr. Francis A. Channing, the son of Dr. Channing's nephew, the Rev. W. H. Channing, would gladly have been here but for duties connected with a county election, which leave him the only alternative of being present with us heartily in spirit. (The President's remark here that a daughter of the Rev. W. H. Channing, Mrs. Edwin Arnold, was present, was received with cordial welcome by the meeting.) After thanking the Committee most warmly for organizing this commemoration, Mr. Channing continues:—"Your meeting has my heartiest sympathy, and I wish I could join you in publicly paying my own tribute of praise to my great relative. It is well that we should take such an opportunity to refresh our memories of one whose passionate love of truth and liberty was only equalled by his gentleness and generosity of spirit. Channing was neither a mystic nor a *doctrinaire*. He was above all things a man, and it was in the assertion of the inherent divinity of human nature, that the strong point of his Idealism lay. It is just this, too, that made him a reverent reformer. His broad human sympathies made him protest against tyranny, whether spiritual or material, but his protests were ever tempered with maganimity, and with a sympathetic appreciation for what was humanly good even in what he opposed. So we find him looking for good rather than prying into evil. He was the soul of the reaction against the stern theology of the Puritans, but it was in warmth and breadth of assertion that he showed his strength, not in bitterness of negation. His temper was above controversy. If he broke down barriers it was not for the pleasure of breaking them, but for the joy of openness and freedom. So too of his style. Its purity and simplicity were the reflection of a singular directness and clearness of thought. Its source was that same open-minded and wholesome humanity, which was the central principle of his nature and his life. To look back to Channing's words is a comfort, too, to those who believe in human progress despite the ebb and flow which from time to time puzzle our vision. When one watches, as I have been doing, at the great political meetings of the hour, the eager and intelligent faces of thousands of sons of toil, and when one discerns how much political rights and national education have done for them in the last fifty years, those noble lectures on the Elevation of the Labouring Classes come vividly again before one. Still more vividly have I been reminded of the spirit of Channing's teaching, when I have heard these thousands generously and earnestly applauding the words of those who have denounced unjust and cruel wars as dishonourable to our country. We can easily exaggerate Channing's realized achievements, but we cannot easily exaggerate the beautiful intensity of his faith, nor the transparent truthfulness of his aspirations. His was a pure and tender light which shone afar into the years to come, for shewing in love and hope the possibilities of human nature."—The REV. DR. EDWIN A. ABBOTT writes:—"I very much regret that the state of my health will prevent me from being present at the forthcoming Centenary Commemoration of Dr. Channing; and my knowledge of his life and works is too slight, I am sorry to say, to enable me to write anything of sufficient weight to deserve attention at so important a gathering. Nevertheless I shall always feel grateful for your invitation, because it led me to the study of his works. What I have read increases my regret at my enforced absence. But I hope many more worthy representatives of the Church of England will be present to testify that in the contemplation of Channing's simple allegiance and loyal devotion to Christ it is impossible even for us Trinitarians not to derive a spiritual benefit, and to feel that even as regards the worship of Christ we have much to learn from the study of the words and and works of so true a servant of our common Master.

But what has most impressed me has been the thorough and systematic manner in which this great Prophet of Reform applied the principles of Christi anity to social and political questions. It is here, most of all, that we of the Church of England must feel that in Channing we have a pattern whom we shall do well to keep before our minds for many generations: and for my part, after reading his discourses on Slavery and on the Abolitionists, and contrasting his political theory and practice with that of many of my brethren in the English Church, I am tempted to wish that there might be added to our Thirty Nine Articles yet a Fortieth, teaching our clergy to distinguish between that lower form of politics which he describes as "the tactics of party for gaining power" and that higher form which he defines as "the study and pursuit of the true enduring good of a community, and the application of great, unchangeable principles to public affairs"—which latter pursuit no minister of Christ can neglect with spiritual impunity. More especially in his discourses on the Elevation of the Labouring Classes I know not who can fail to sympathize with his high yet sober ideal of the future in store for working men; with his anticipations of the powerful part that Christianity is destined to play in bringing about that brighter state of things to come; and with his indignant protest that the future influence of Christianity must not be judged from its effect in these past periods in which it has been perverted to a political engine for making the poor poorer, and for preventing the meek from inheriting the earth. If one result of this Centenary Commmemoration should be to circulate among our working men these discourses of Dr. Channing's, no slight step may perhaps have been taken towards that new application of Christian principles, for which this great teacher and philanthropist contended as a veritable and essential part of Christianity itself."—The REV. DR. STOUGHTON after explaining that he could not return from his visit to Italy in time for this meeting, says:—" Dr. Channing was to me, when a youth, a favourite author, and though, of course I did not accept some of his theological conclusions, yet I derived from some of his discourses much spiritual profit and enjoyment. They had an elevating and purifying effect, which I hope never to lose: and there is a passage in his sermon on the Character of Christ, which I have often quoted in the pulpit, and which now recurs to me in my solitude, with a peculiar charm, as I think of those who are gone, and of that Blessed Saviour who has taken them to Himself: " He lives and reigns, and with a clear calm faith I see Him in that state of glory, and I confidently expect, at no distant period, to see Him face to face. *We have indeed no absent friend whom we shall so surely meet.*" Dr. Channing's advocacy of Negro Emancipation, when the name of it was cast out as evil, and the cause in America was trampled under foot, awakened my warmest enthusiasm; and in his just views of war, and its accompaniments of differents kinds—deceitful show, false splendour, and unreal glory, as well as slaughter and ruin, I fully sympathized. His thoughts on " Ministry for the poor " " the Sunday School " " the Obligations of a city to care for and watch over the moral health of its members "—these bore a high value in my estimation, and were often pondered by me in early days, when engaged in arduous pastoral work. Of the literary merits of his works I could also say much; albeit that they sometimes appear almost lost amidst the moral and spiritual beauty and greatness of his life. When I was in Boston a few years ago, I had means of judging how great was the influence he exercised there; and the tone of religious feeling—I should call it evangelical—which I witnessed in some on whom his mantle had fallen, called forth from me the warmest response."—The REV. DR. RALEIGH, though unhappily too ill to be present, wished his name to be mentioned as sympathizing heartily in the object of the meeting. He says:—" It would give me great pleasure to join the friends who are purposing to honour the memory and character of the late Dr. Channing, and to remind the world of the great services he rendered to the cause of "civil and religious liberty," and to the many specific movements which that general phrase involves, some of which in his day had few friends. More than forty years ago, when I was hardly more than a lad, the perusal of some of his writings gave my mind one of the most powerful and freshening impulses it has ever received, and one of the most lasting, for I believe that what I then received has mingled congenially and wholesomely with later thoughts and with some of my deepest convictions."—A telegraph message was then read from the Protestant Union of Germany, to this effect:—" The Executive Committee of the German Protestantenverein sends its cordial good wishes for the celebration of the 100th birthday of Dr. William Ellery Channing, the great modern apostle of the true humanity of Jesus, the defender of the rights of man against slavery in Church and State. May his ideas penetrate the communities of the old and new worlds, and unite them in one great Christian church according to the Channing ideal."

From Iceland the REV. M. JOCHUMSSON wrote:—
" Having been so often and generously aided and encouraged by the Committee of the B. & F. U. Association in my humble endeavour to advance among my countrymen higher and purer Christian and moral views, especially those of W. E. Channing, and being not permitted to join you personally, I feel it simply my duty to express my most heartfelt sympathy with all those who on the 7th of the next April celebrate the commemoration of that great and good man.

" Ten years are gone since the day I first happened to see the name and the works of Channing, and almost immediately I felt I had met with a spiritual guide for life. Ever since I have become more and more convinced of this great man's special power to meet the deepest spiritual wants of our age, not only in his capacity of an ingenious preacher of pure and rational Christianity, but as a new Prophet and Reformer for coming generations! I know no author so full of *charity*—charity may be the secret of his mission. And often when reading his beautiful discourses I have been questioning myself, why is not this man more universally accepted The full daytime of his fame, the full harvest-time of his work is yet to come. In presenting this humble testimony before the illustrious assembly of his Centenary Commemoration, I have no warmer wish to utter, no warmer prayer to offer, than that every country and every soul might soon become acquainted with the Work and Genius of William Ellery Channing. I am glad to add that a large and ever-increasing number of my younger countrymen join me in the same congratulation. All hail to the spirit of W. E. Channing from the *Ultima Thule*."

WILLIAM RATHBONE, Esq., being unable to attend the meeting as he had promised and hoped to do, wrote :—
"It is most unfortunate that the Channing Centenary should fall in the midst of a General Election. Many will be prevented from being present who yet feel, as I do, that they owe to the teaching of Dr. Channing much of their hatred of what is base and untrue, and their enthusiasm for all that tends to make man what he ought to be. I see some stress is laid upon Dr. Channing being a Unitarian. This is, I think, a mistake. Dr. Channing himself said that he never would shrink from the name of Unitarian so long as it was used as a term of opprobrium, but he did not love such terms of sectarian distinction. He was simply, and above all things, a Christian; and, therefore, above all those distinctions which separate, alas, too frequently, the adherents of our common faith. It is for this reason that I revere him, and acknowledge him as my teacher; and it is on this ground that we do invite, and have a right to invite, the sympathy and co-operation of our fellow-Christians in our admiration of him, even though they may not belong to the same division of the Christian army. It

was to the single eye with which he applied these principles, and to the undoubting faith with which he advocated them, that we owe what I think to be one of the most wonderful achievements of honest remonstrance—I mean the effect of his letter upon the contemplated annexation of Texas by the American people. That remonstrance checked for a time the course of a nation bent upon an unlawful conquest in an unlawful cause, and, though the evil spirit returned to its prey again, and the wrong was done which, in my opinion, made the Civil War in America inevitable, no one can, I think, doubt that the good seed remained, though buried for a time, and that the opinions and feeling which grew from that seed have contributed in no small degree to the emancipation of England's great offspring from the curse of slavery—a curse which tainted the whole political life of a people to whom the whole world looks to show what Freedom can do with opportunities so magnificent and aspirations so generous as our American offspring possess."

The Rev. Dr. MARTINEAU: May I venture to say one word on behalf of the Dean of Westminster? I the more readily spoke to him about this meeting some weeks ago, because he had told me that when he was in America he believed he never preached a single sermon without mentioning the honoured name of Channing. I knew, therefore, that he felt an interest in the works and in the life of Channing. When this occasion was named to him he took it up with great interest, entered it in his diary as an engagement, and most fully intended to be with us this night. But afterwards I had a letter from him, in which he explained that a very unusual pressure of work having considerably broken him down and unfitted him for the pressure of the season coming on in London, he found it was absolutely necessary for him to secure a short interval of rest in the country. The only days that were at his disposal for that purpose were, unfortunately, precisely the days including this meeting. He is now in the island of Guernsey for the sake of a little refreshment, and he begs me to explain this matter; and he trusts that neither within nor without the limits of the Church, will his absence be misunderstood.

The CHAIRMAN :—Ladies and Gentlemen, We have assembled here this evening to celebrate the Centenary of the birth of that man of venerated memory, Dr. William Ellery Channing, and we may feel that in this endeavour to pay homage where so much admiration and gratitude are due, we are joining with thousands who are now meeting in other lands and in far distant places to celebrate the event. They are refreshing, as we hope to do, their minds and hearts with deep draughts from the well of his intense religious devotion at these memorial meetings. We welcome with outstretched cordial hands all lovers of Channing from whatever church or communion they may come; for in all churches and climes good men are to be found who know and revere and love the name of Channing. His words and his works are cosmopolitan and for all time. They are words of love and reverence and wisdom concerning the Eternal Father of mankind, and of man as God's child and our brother, wherever he may be found. And it is in this spirit of our great Exemplar Christ, in whose steps Channing so humbly, so lovingly, so confidingly walked, that we welcome all here to-night to assist in honouring this truly great, this wonderfully God-loving man, and to do what may in us lie to extend still wider and more fully the knowledge and appreciation of his works and of the spirit of their author. We shall thus fulfil the cherished wish of his life to extend more fully this influence and make it a common property, universal everywhere—that ennobling, glorious, intense consciousness of the Deity that he felt as the loving parent, the support and, at the same time, the reason of man's existence. If for a moment we look back over the pages of history to the surroundings of Channing this day hundred years, and consider the progress which the more educated and refined portion of the world has made since then, politically, morally, socially, and religiously, we see and feel the effect that Channing and scores of God-loving, God-fearing men like him, have had in purifying and ennobling their race; and may feel well strengthened by the knowledge of that progress to strive to keep it alive and growing. The poet says, and I cannot help thinking that there is great force in his words :—

> "Where is the victory of the grave?
> What dust upon the spirit lies?
> God keeps the sacred life he gave;
> The prophet never dies."

DR. MARTINEAU'S ADDRESS.

MR. PRESIDENT AND FRIENDS,

If I accept the place assigned me here this evening, it is because I have experienced three-fourths of the Century we are assembled to survey, and have fresh in my memory the first emergence of Channing's name. But it is not all advantage that old age brings to me here: for if its retrospect is long, its debt is heavy; and I know not how to compress sixty years of gratitude within half-an-hour's speech. My duty will be most compendiously performed if, without dwelling on any special aspect of Channing's many-sided wisdom, I first glance rapidly at the Biography of his mind; and then draw forth from it the central Principle, the living inspiration, which pervaded it throughout, and made it a simple and homogeneous power.

In reviewing the life of a distinguished man, it is easy to ascribe too much to the scene and incidents of his early years. Rhode Island has interesting features, natural and historical, which were very dear to Channing, and doubtless formed him as the world forms all of us: but for neither its bright skies and picturesque surface, nor for the memories of Berkeley that linger round its "Hanging Rocks," shall I claim any distinctive influence. There were many children born at Newport in those days, without becoming Channings; and it were fanciful to see his characteristics inscribed on the alcoves, or hear his future in the waves upon the beach. Often however it is from local incidents very small in the eyes of others that children receive their most permanent impressions : and scarcely any one of Channing's leading enthusiasms is without some significant presage in his boyish experience : *e.g.*

Slavery was familiar to his native place, not only by recent usage, but by the merchants of Newport being still engaged (like those of Bristol and Liverpool) in the African Slave-trade : and no social sentiment was yet awakened against it, even in Channing's home. But there was a minister there of Puritan faithfulness and courage, Dr. Hopkins,—a pupil of Jonathan Edwards,—whose eyes had been opened to the iniquity, and who unflinchingly preached against it. The conflict of sentiment which thus stirred the air of the town, and gave a black and guilty look to certain of the ships in its harbour, struck upon the heart of the boy, and prevented that sleep of the imagination upon mere custom which is the source of half the cruelties in the world.

Another branch of the local commerce was in the wines of Europe and the rum of the West Indies, and encouraged habits of indulgence mischievous to the moral life. Abstinence Societies were still a generation off. But one solitary voice made itself heard on behalf of severe *Temperance*,—that of a Baptist Preacher,— *Father Thurston*,—who enforced his word by an eccentric testimony. His ministry left him so poor that on week-days he worked for his living as a *journeyman-*

cooper. But nothing could induce him to have anything to do with barrels and puncheons to accommodate spirituous drinks: and he kept himself from sin by making nothing but water-buckets:—surely, a picturesque, though whimsical protest on behalf of Temperance, never to be forgotten by the fancy and conscience of a sensitive boy!

The sequence of the French Revolution upon the American was one of *sympathy* as well as *time*, and commenced that close relation between Paris and Washington which has often touched our national jealousy. Every reader of Channing must have remarked how little he shared his compatriots' admiration for French models and French ideas of political life. The intense aversion with which he regarded the desolating rapacity of Napoleon was but the prolonged shock which he caught from his father's look and voice on hearing of the execution of Louis XVI. in 1793. The horrors which culminated in that act dissipated all hopes of any noble liberty for Europe under the lead of such missionaries. And from that hour his heart turned back to England as the true asylum of law-abiding freedom, and his face was firmly set against the fatal illusions which he designated as "*French principles*," and their daring excuses for military conquest.

With equal precision do we alight in his boyhood on his first revolt from the *sternness of the prevailing Theology*. A great preacher, whom his father had driven him some miles to hear, so terribly painted the endless torment of sinners and the paucity of the saved, as to steep the boy's whole soul in sadness and dread,--which were deepened as he heard his father say to some one "Sound doctrine, Sir!" As they drove home, with the shadow still upon his heart and the feeling that it covered the whole of life,—his father began whistling; and, when they arrived, instead of telling the story with bated breath, hurried off his boots, flung himself into an easy chair, and read the newspaper! Could he help feeling that the unseen flames had not the reality for others that they had for him? Did he not gain his first insight into the self-deceptions of religious fiction? He might not yet understand how, to the preacher, those pictured horrors had perhaps become but pulpit fire-works, and to the hearer but a secondary flash in the mirror of thought: but somehow, they did not seem to be believed, as he reckoned belief. It is not when the real voice of God is sounding, that men whistle and look up the news; but only when the thunder has rolled away into echoes, and echoes of echoes, till it dies into a reminiscence of they know not what. Channing was incapable of religion at second-hand: it was identical in him with the very focus of his nature.

And that focus, he always said, was first reached by the appeals and exercises of a *Revival* period at New London, when he was thirteen years of age. It was not that he was then snatched through any violent transition. His "whole life," he declares, was occupied by the "process of Conversion." But he then was brought, consciously and permanently, into the presence of

Divine relations, and dedicated himself to serve, only and utterly, the will of God.

In this state of mind it was,—called to the devout life, repelled from severe Calvinism, with sympathies bespoken against Slavery, against " French Principles," and on behalf of Temperance and Moral Reform,—that he entered his four College years (1794-8). For every generous youth, gifted with any wealth of faculty, this is a glorious time,—the blossoming season of mind and heart, whose sunshine and showers can never be forgotten, but still spread their green memories through the winter of age. Besides this charm of general growth, the Harvard years added to Channing two large elements of inward power.

Apart from all direct religious development, his true genius found him out; not only by winning him for historical and literary studies, in preference to mathematics and philosophy; but by giving him over in complete captivity to the *Ethics of Disinterestedness* taught by Hutcheson, and politically applied by Ferguson. To this system his whole soul responded with an ecstasy of enthusiasm that became more and more rapt for many a year. It was useless for a Hartley or a Helvetius to preach the originality and supremacy of Self-love to affections like his; or for Absolutist theologians, in presence of a conscience like his, to resolve right and wrong into arbitrary decrees of the Divine Will. He knew the possibility, the obligation, the privilege, of living for others, of free self-sacrifice, of identification with God's infinite love; and, once possessed of this knowledge, could never be persuaded to give humanity a lower aim.

The wave of French irreligion, which seemed to be flooding the whole literature of the time, carried him to a deliberate study of the *Evidences and Characteristics of Christianity*. And here it was that he "found what he was made for." It was a repetition, at a sublimer level, of his experience with Hutcheson's philosophy, and brought into harmonious relation his theory of Man and the Revelation of God in Christ. His resolve was taken at once to devote himself to the Christian Ministry, as the highest form of service to mankind, and the nearest station to the Fountain of all truth and good. And lest any one, judging from the somewhat haggard features of the published portraits, should think that in this fervid growth of his nature there was some morbid and feverish intensity, it may be well to add that, through all this time, his health was robust, his strength —for his small figure—was that of an athlete, and his spirits were lively and joyous : so that the bases of his character and convictions were laid upon a physical ground firm and clear.

From the stimulating scenes of University life he was thrown, for nearly two years (1798-1800), into almost utter loneliness, as a Tutor and Schoolmaster in Virginia. It was a memorable, in some respects a disastrous, period in his experience. His thoughts, his vows, his enthusiasms, no longer drawn forth and aired in congenial society, turned inwards in meditation, and with incandescent heat consumed his store of bodily strength, and, inducing an ascetic habit, enfeebled the vigour of all his remaining years. He pushed his explorations however in one new direction. So long as he was surrounded by companions and felt the ferment of the world around him, he had reflected chiefly on the Individual Soul in its relation to God. Now that he is in virtual solitude, he is drawn to the contemplation of *Social problems:* he becomes accessible to the benevolent visions of the European Revolution: he is fascinated by the brilliant dreams of Rousseau, of Godwin and Mary Wollstonecraft, and by the Pantisocracy of Coleridge and Southey. Stung by daily contact with Slavery and its vices, he is pierced to the heart by the woes and wrongs of human Society, and listens to every reasoned promise of juster and happier days. In one sense, these Social Prophets make a convert of him: he believes in their *end;* but he does not believe in their *means.* He has no trust in political revolutions and reconstructions, in a new-birth of the whole without regeneration of the parts, in peace and equity upon an earth unconscious of the Eternal Righteousness in heaven. His Social speculations are all baptized in his Christian ideal: they involve the sanctification of men, taken one by one ; and, at his touch, the secular golden age turns into the " Kingdom of God."

From Virginia he issued, like St. Paul from Arabia, with his Gospel essentially complete, and ready to be tested by contact with the thoughts and life of men. But feeble health and eager reading still detained him from his public work till, in 1803, he entered into that connection with the Federal St. Church in Boston, which continued for 38 out of his 40 remaining years; viz., twenty years of sole ministry (1803-22); and sixteen (1824-40) of colleagueship with Gannett, divided by two years (1822-24) of absence in Europe. If I hasten over these momentous decades in a few sentences, it is not because the story of his spiritual growth is over, but simply that henceforth its type was determined; it took on no new members; it became symmetrical and rose into grace and grandeur in all its dimensions at once: and the forty years fall into sections, not by inward changes, but by outward differences of opportunity for the application of his spirit to human life.

The first section,—prior to his European visit,—is interesting chiefly as having *defined his Theology*. It was not a task particularly congenial to him. His intellect was not mechanical and systematic, requiring to map out the 'sphere of Religion into latitudes and longitudes and fit a truth into every square. He could have been well content to let the New England Churches that had relaxed their Puritan rigour go on with their indeterminate or latitudinarian mood of mind in which he found them for the first ten or twelve years of his ministry. When he came to think of it, he "had never really been either Trinitarian or Calvinist"; yet he was indebted for much of his deepest trust and piety to those who were; and from them he would never spontaneously sever himself, so long as they would hold communion with him. But that time had come to an end. The sweet airs of neutral music that had hitherto sufficed to harmonize the religious host of Boston and "charm into a beauteous frame," were now suspected and denounced as beguiling temptations; and the theological trumpet was seized for lips that blew no "uncertain sound" and summoned the field to divide itself off for battle. At first, Channing was content with protesting against "the system of exclusion and denunciation." But a journal being established ("The Panoplist"), for the express purpose of assailing the modern doctrines and excommunicating their professors, self-defence became inevitable, and faithfulness demanded the plainest declaration of conviction. He took part in this controversy with the decision and fervour which he threw into every duty. But his doctrinal period was short (1819-26): he compressed its work into three or four striking discourses; and, having borne his testimony, returned to mingle with the Universal Church, and, whether owned or disowned by others, still strove to reach and touch the garment of Christ.

If any one might have been expected to thrust him aside from that healing contact and say he had no business there, it was S. T. Coleridge, who by that time had found so many contemptuous words to heap on the heresy he once had preached. Yet the personal presence of Channing, when he visited England in 1822, quite won the heart of the philosopher, and led him to declare that Channing "loved the good as the good and the true as the truth, with that harmonious subordination of the latter to the former, without encroachment on the absolute worth of either, which present a character that in my heart's heart I believe to be the very rarest on earth." It would have been interesting to know what impression he left on Wordsworth also, whom he visited at Rydal. But a large part of their conversation was held under conditions not favourable to authentic record. Channing, staying at Grasmere, and being out of health, had engaged a vehicle to make his call. The Poet, it is well known, was always at his best *in a walk*, and, after a little time in the house, proposed to accompany Channing back to his inn on foot. Channing, becoming exhausted within the first half-mile, begged that they might ride the rest of the way. And so they did. But as the vehicle was a *one-horse cart* (the only thing to be had), and the mountain roads were not smooth in those pre-Macadamite days, the situation was not the most eligible for a Platonic dialogue, and their speculations would be shaken by the ruts into a very fragmentary philosophy.

Returning from his European journey, he entered on the second and last section of his Boston ministry. It opened with the period of his *Great Essays*—on Milton, Napoleon, and Fénelon—disclosing his ideal of individual character; on National Literature and Life, holding forth the true ends of the Commonwealth; on Associations, warning against the encroachments on *personal* life of mechanized action and moral averages, and on the functions of the Christian Ministry in an age when religion must either embrace and consecrate all human interests, or itself dwindle into insignificance. Later on

D

(1830-39) we reach the period of his public action and his civic Manifestoes on Slavery. I must not touch upon the conflicts of that time. They form the scenes of an impressive drama which will be presented to you by one whose generous sympathies will let none of its noble features escape. I will only say that, the hotter the strife, the more did Channing's intrepidity rise, and the calmer did his faith in the right issue become. Till the day of deliverance should come for his own land he exulted in the English liberation of the West Indian slaves, and on successive anniversaries of that First of August delivered animating addresses in commemoration of its "glorious triumph of Christianity and happy augury for the future." The last of these, within a few weeks of his death, was thrown off, as he says, "under the inspiration of the mountains which, you know, are the Holy Land of liberty;" and truly it breathes the air of a rare elevation and commands the sweep of a wide horizon. It was the culmination of a mood which for two or three years had been gaining ascendency in him, and turning his faith into joy, as if he "beheld Satan, as lightning, fall from heaven." He had opened his ministry in plaintive and pathetic tones, touched indeed with the enthusiasm of hope, but saddened by both the grievances of men and his own shortcomings. Ere he closed it the weight was lifted off. He had conquered his despondencies, not by thinking less tenderly of others or less humbly of himself, for never was his love so quick or his ideal so high; but by the triumph of an assured trust and the vision of an Eternal Goodness.

"Perfection," he exclaims, "is revealed to us, not to torture us from our falling short of it, but to be a kindling object to be seized by faith as our destiny, if we are faithful to the light and strength now given." He was even surprised at his own gladness of heart. "What mysteries," he says, "we are to ourselves! Here am I finding life a sweeter cup as I approach to what are called the dregs, looking round on this fair glorious creation with a serener love, and finding more to hope for society at the very time that its evils weigh more upon my mind." Such was the spirit in which he looked his last on the green mountains of Vermont in the autumn of 1842. At sundown of October 2, while he lay with his face turned to the glow upon the hills, he passed away, as if in pursuit of the light he could not quit, and entered that "Perfect Life" which had ever moved before his thought, and of which he left us the prophecy and the fore-gleam. Who can withhold the prayer that *so* may the "Father of lights"—

> "Glorify for us the West,
> When we shall sink to final rest!"

In reviewing the history of this pure and powerful soul, it is easy, from its transparent simplicity, to alight upon the animating principle which constituted its unity and harmony throughout. The single thought of which, from first to last, it was the living expression is this, that MORAL PERFECTION IS THE ESSENCE OF GOD AND THE SUPREME END FOR MAN; in the one, an eternal reality; in the other, a continuous possibility; in both, the ground of perpetual spiritual communion. This was the haunting conception that possessed and moulded the whole mind of Channing: the conception, not of *Morality* in the mere *Social* sense, of a rule of conduct between man and man; or, in the *Negative* sense, of a repressive law, saying of this or that "Thou shalt *not;*" but of *Moral Excellence* in the *Divine and Positive* sense, of an ever-active sway of best affections, an eternal life of holy will, an infinitude of spiritual beauty and love for the true and good, inherent always in the Father of spirits, and open to the approaches of all his children. You can see at once how this faith must spread out its influence in all directions and become the determining power in every field of a man's thought and feeling. Thus:

His *Theology* becomes subject to a paramount *moral critique*, and will allow nothing to be affirmed of God which either revolts or divides the allegiance of the moral nature, and nothing to be denied of Him which is needful for unconditional worship.

His *Ethics* must recognize in every man the conditions of a *progressive moral life, i.e.*, potential knowledge of the Right, and power over it; and treat the capacity for duty and self-devotion as the supreme glory of our nature, apart from which all its other adornments, intellect, genius, unregulated Will, are but mutilated splendours. Hence he will draw his tests of *true and false greatness*, to guide him in his reading of literature and history; and his judgments of personal vices, whether in past or present characters. And as all offences against right must appear to him, not merely as *failures*, but as breaches of *trust*, and all high excellence as the fruit of *faithfulness*, he will speak of them, not with the acquiescent or pleased acceptance which he would give to a squally or a sunny day, but with the expostulating censure and enthusiastic homage of a soul not afraid of its own reverence and sorrow and righteous anger.

When he thinks of what *Society and the State* should be and do, he will condemn as *wrongs* whatever needlessly *hinders or suppresses the mental and moral capacities of any class*, be it ignorance that might be removed, or servitude that might be abolished, or poverty that might be rendered less crushing, or the wasteful resort to force in controversies amenable to reason and the sense of right. In every such case he will demand redress for the neglected souls of men, and stand up as their Tribune in the forum of humanity, undismayed by the frowns of the world's dictators.

You see, too, why it is that he will distrust the agency of organized sects and associations, except for the occasional accomplishment of some external work. For *Moral Perfection*—the supreme end of human life—is not *collective*, but *individual*, the separate aspiration of all souls, taken one by one, the aim with which " no stranger intermeddleth," and which lives only as a secret understanding with our God. And the more we club together and fill our days with action in groups and crowds, the more do we silence the highest voices within us, and accept the low average of good which can secure the votes of all.

And do you think he can despond of the *Future of mankind?* Is it not guaranteed for progress by the very constitution of their nature? Is the Reason which is the possibility of truth, the Conscience which is the organ of right, and the nameless faculty which tends to all beauty and spiritual good, to be for ever abortive with countless millions of our race? No! the *Inner capacity* will beat the *outward hindrances* at last: for it is constant, while they are variable, and by its persistent pressure will drive them from the field and throw open the advent of better days.

And still more must he hope for the *Future of the Individual soul.* Made as it is in the likeness of God, with powers indefinitely exceeding its temporal opportunities, with affections that commune with the Infinitely Good and can rest in nothing less, it carries in it the signs of immortality, the ineffaceable relations to the Everlasting life and love.

Thus, by the simplest expansion of Channing's Primary Thought, Duty becomes supreme over the personal life; Reverence, over the social; Aspiration, over the spiritual; and Love for the true, the beautiful, and the good, over all.

It is not surprising that, with this vital tissue running through the whole sphere of his conceptions, we come again and again upon the same great thoughts, whatever may be the subject of which he treats. Whether he follows the armies of Napoleon, or looks with Tuckerman into the garrets of the Boston poor; whether he converses with the saintly Fénelon, or lectures to a

Mechanics' Institute, or addresses a Southern slave-holder, or ordains a New England minister, you will not listen long to his discourse without recognizing tones which you have heard from him before. The greatness of the soul; Christ, as the standard of humanity and the uplifter to God; the solemn authority of the conscience; the achievements possible to spiritual energy; these are topics to which he often recurs, and from which, as from a prism, he can throw light of different hues and in various directions. Does this frequent resort to a commanding principle indicate poverty of resource? Is any one inconsiderate enough to complain of it as a tiresome repetition? As well might he complain of a writer on the Theory of Mechanics wearying him with the Law of Gravitation. It is the special excellence of a true and great formula that there is no end to the cases which it will resolve; and he that has a key to unlock the largest number of problems stands at the highest altitude of intelligence.

Yes, if it be indeed a *true* formula. But what, I may be asked, if it be but a sublime illusion? Then, the more comprehensive it is, the more terrible will be the sweep of its disappointment. M. Renan speaks of it as Channing's "untiring optimism*," in that tone of placid indulgence with which modern criticism looks down on the most opposite human phenomena as all very proper in their time. If this be all, I know not why we should be here, at this late date, to celebrate a

---

* Optimisme infatigable. *See* Études sur l'histoire religieuse, p. 372.

bygone faith and try to reanimate its power. Were it but the happy trance of individual fancy, now dispersed, it would be a waste of time to recite in the morning the dreams that have vanished with the night. *We*, who are assembled here in homage to Channing, mean, I presume, to re-affirm that faith of his, in Moral Perfection as the essence of God's nature and the Goal of ours, and to put our trust in its living efficacy. I know of nothing that contradicts it but our blindness and sloth of heart. Has it not the inner witness of all the greatest and highest souls? nay, of him, the unique representative of our humanity, who called us to be "Perfect as the Father in heaven is perfect"? Does it not meet with a large and deep response from consciences far less exalted, when appealed to by a faithful and penetrating voice? Have not the writings of Channing elicited that response from thousands who never so realized before the moral trust committed to them, the divine glory of duty and self-sacrifice, and their indefinite capacities of thought and affection? And has it not the evidence of its Practical Energy in the world? What else has kindled the heroism and breathed the patience, to face the appalling sins and sorrows of men, and seek the downcast that have none to help them? Where, but for this, would have been our Howards and Clarksons and Garrisons, our Florence Nightingale, and Sister Dora, and Mary Carpenter, and Josephine Butler? This faith is the source of all missions of persuasive love, of all saintly lives, of all hope on either side of death. And it is endowed with a magic power of fulfilling its own prophecies. Just as you may often *create* a goodness in another by simply trusting and expecting it; so, when you speak to the world's heart as if, like your own, it had shame for its sins and sighs after the Infinite Righteousness, you will bring the sorrow and the yearning though they were not there before, and realize your own assumption. A faith which is believed because it is true, may also become more true because it is believed.

I know that this trust in Moral Perfection, always resisted by our lower nature, is habitually treated as romance by the cynical spirit of our time. The Pessimist,—now the favourite of fashion,—gleans up the miseries so thickly strewn around, and plants them as a canker to gnaw away the very heart of hope. He reminds us how hard is the struggle of life to the mass of men, how faint the trace in them of any but gross and selfish aims. He lays bare the hideous vices of our boasted civilization,—the barbarities of war, the frauds of commerce, the hypocrisies of diplomacy, the vanities of society: and when he has led us through his museum of abominations, he asks us whether about this pest-house of a world any such great things can be said. I believe that this kind of appeal has thrown a heavy weight of anxiety on the heart of our age, and marked lines of sadness on many an earnest face. In this very fact, however,—if you will bear with the paradox,—I find relief. Why does the dark picture affect us with such grief? Is it because these dreadful blots compel us to throw away our standard of human nature and drop it down to a level indefinitely lower? On the contrary, if our nature became in our eyes one in which these things were at home and congenial, like ferocity in the hyæna and cunning in the fox, we could see them there and remain at peace. The sorrow which they bring comes from this,—that we cannot bear to see so great a nature in so vile a plight: it is a shock of surprise, a blow of despondency, even a cry of anguish, induced by the felt incongruity between a possible nobleness and an actual degradation; and is itself a confession of ineradicable faith in the soul being made for better things. Great guilt and great woes can have no place in little natures: it is the ruin of mighty powers, the eclipse of glorious lights, that fills us with awe as we gaze on them. If life were not designed for beauty, why be dismayed at its deformities? If goodness were not our end, why shed tears that it is lost? The *tragic* character of all such facts is due to their being a *fall-away* from some eminence that might have been attained or held: and thus the very pathos of Pessimism is lent to it by the faith which it denies.

It is quite possible then for the same mind to have at once the deepest sense of the evils of humanity, and the highest confidences in the resources for surmounting them. And of this combination, once at least perfected in this world, Channing was a touching and even sublime example. No nature could more sensitively recoil from all that is base, impure, or cruel: he had precisely the temperament which would dispose him to fastidious exaggeration of all blemishes in character and life. And assuredly he did not ignore the "ugly facts" of human experience; for who has more forcibly and fearfully presented them? yet with him these actualities on the front of our humanity are as nothing compared with the possibilities in reserve. No sin frightened his vision of Holiness; no death, his assurance of Immortality. To him, the saddest phenomena were but the mask of a hidden beauty and greatness behind. He could not bear the whinings of despondency, the prophecies of ruin, which were becoming current among the languid and passive critics in the cultured world around him : "those whose duty it is to carry forwards Society," he said, "despair of it. They despair of the body of the people, despair of our institutions, despair of liberty throughout the world. Too many of our young men grow up in a school of despair." "For my part, I have been disappointed in friends and public men, but I place unshaken reliance on the grand results of Providence." "Amid human inconstancy and guilt, I know that God has still devout servants on earth, and that truth, piety, and goodness are immortal and will prevail." And so " I find life an increasing good,—more beautiful and glorious,—and the human race more and more interesting." "Lord now lettest thou thy servant depart in peace."

The intensity of Channing's faith has so penetrated his words, that they seem to carry in them a living fire. Still more perhaps is this feature manifest in his constant feeling of their inadequacy. "I wish I had power" (he repeatedly says) "to give you some new conviction of the greatness of this truth."—" How can I bring home to you this perfection of the soul as the supreme good?" "O for a voice of power," he exclaims, "to arouse the human spirit from its death in life, and quicken it with the consciousness of its own nature!" Such was his perpetual sigh and prayer. And may we not say, that the prayer has been answered? If all whom his word has awakened to that consciousness could at this moment send their witness into this hall, should we not stand in presence of a mighty chorus of the living and the dead? Would the response come only from his native land? Would it be delivered only in the English tongue? Would it not turn this day into a day of Pentecost, and be heard in every European language from Iceland to Italy? And does it not then justify our celebration, and crown it with a thankful joy, that " He, being dead, *thus* speaketh " ?

THE REV. J. BALDWIN BROWN'S ADDRESS.

The brief paper which I have undertaken to read to you to-night will concern itself entirely with the character and work of Dr. Channing as a spiritual teacher. To that I confine myself, for I understand that the topics have been so distributed as to secure some sort of unity in the business of the evening.

St. Peter little suspected the range of the emancipation of thought and spirit of which he was the instrument, when he "perceived that in every nation he that feareth God and worketh righteousness is accepted with him." God is ever guiding us into the same truth in relation to the creeds, but we have not fully perceived it yet. In truth it is hard work for us, as it was hard work for Peter. But we must master the lesson, or this weak, struggling, distracted condition of the Church will prolong itself to the sorrow and shame of all Christian souls. Few sentences more blighting to the germs which ripen into the fruits of the Spirit have been spoken in Christendom than the celebrated judgment that, "The virtues of the heathen are but splendid vices." These words, and the thought which inspired them, have made the Church the witness against, and not to, the great human world through all the Christian ages; and have filled the sphere of Christian history with bitter enmities and fierce contentions, instead of with a light of Divine love, golden and glorious as dawn, stealing on by gentle and yet triumphant progresses, and at length flooding the earth with the splendour of the perfect day. There can be no question, I fear, that the temptation of the churches is to transfer to the graces of their Christian rivals the judgment once formulated on the virtues of the heathen, and to look coldly and with dark suspicion on the signs of a noble and faithful life outside their own pale. That is, they are tempted to think of themselves and not of their Master; of the credit of their creeds and not of the Saviour. I suppose that one of the chief curses of Christendom in all ages has been man's limitation of the kingdom of Heaven. The Saviour foresaw it. "Nevertheless when the Son of Man cometh will he find faith in the earth?" faith in Him and in His kingdom, and not in the parodies of it which man may set up in its stead, to mock the longing hope of mankind.

One of the best and most hopeful features of the times in which we live, is the measure in which this perception of Peter is spreading among Christians. The Churches are keen for their creeds still, and they are bound to be keen. I am not here to-night because I think lightly of the doctrinal belief which I hold in God manifest in the flesh. Our creeds, if they are worth anything, are something more than intellectual beliefs; they are modes of apprehending and realizing vital facts which are deeply related to the noble and fair unfolding of the life. Life gathers its tone and tinge from what it feeds on, and we are bound to contend strenuously for what we believe to be the truth of God in the doctrine and discipline of the Christian Church. But the Churches are opening the eyes of their understandings to see that there is one thing greater than their creeds, a Christ-like life, and to recognize and honour it wherever it may appear; nor are they startled and perplexed, as they once were, if they find it in a very pure and noble form quite outside their own pale.

Two things, I think, among many others, are found very helpful to this happy result. The first is, the tremendous trial through which our common Christianity is passing. I will not call it a deadly trial, for it is well that we should remember that there is nothing in God's truth which can die, or even be in danger of dying; but still, the trial is a searching one. The second is, great Christian lives, of which a very noble typical example is that of William Ellery Channing. The assault on Christianity in these days is so determined, and so aimed at that which is most vital, that the lovers of the truth are drawn—I will not say driven —into closer fellowship by the apparent peril of that which they hold most dear. The time of danger and pressure always brings out the unity in communities, and shows the diversities in their real proportions. "Blood is thicker than water," said the American captain when he saw us hard pressed in China, and gallantly struck into the fray on our side. It was esteemed an omen of doom in the death struggle of the Jews that their deadly peril inflamed instead of mitigating their intestine hates. We are banded together not to defend —the truth wants less defence than we think—but to maintain the truth of the Gospel; and we rejoice, as we stand shoulder to shoulder, to find how much in heart and life we are one. I say the truth wants less defence than we think. We are not God's advocates, we are His witnesses. Speak the truth, live the truth, and cease your panics: it will defend and advocate itself. But there can be no doubt that the assault which is now directed on the very foundations of the faith, tends to band believers together in loving and holy fellowship. And it is not only the essentials of Christianity which are assailed, it is the essentials of humanity; the presence of a spirit in man, as well as the presence of a God in nature—a being with whom man can hold living communion; whose thoughts he can think out after him, and whose presence will be the bliss of his heaven.

And here I am thankful to be able to acknowledge publicly, on behalf of a great company, the deep debt of gratitude which we owe to your distinguished scholar and preacher, Dr. Martineau, for his noble and conclusive vindications of the reality of that spiritual sphere, without whose experiences, aspirations, and hopes men would find, in the long run, that life was not worth the living; and then suicide would again rise to the dignity of an art, as it did in the days of Imperial Rome. I think that some effectual part of Dr. Channing's mantle rests on Dr. Martineau. The essential dignity of man was the key-note of the deepest passages of his writings —the dignity of man and the love of God, which is an essential part of that dignity; and it is precisely the spiritual dignity of man which Dr. Martineau has upheld with such convincing power against the philosophy, falsely so called, which would degrade it, and set it in the dust.

The wisest Christian teacher whom I have ever known—the late A. J. Scott, of Manchester—said some thirty years ago, " A theology that shuts out human interests is teaching men a humanity that shuts out God and Christ." It was a remarkable forecast of what we see around us now. In the last generation the dominant theology deliberately expelled the larger human interests from its sphere, and preached a kingdom of heaven whose principles and methods of administration, when brought out into the sunlight, simply revolted the heart and conscience of mankind. The present generation is striving strenuously to exclude God and Christ from the human sphere, and is bent on trying the experiment whether man's life, and the larger interests and activities of human society, cannot be made to flourish without any religion at all. That is the question which the assize of the "ermine-robed great world" is trying now. We may look on the progress of the experiment, not with composure exactly—the disturbance of sacred beliefs is too serious, the agony of doubt and mental conflict into which earnest minds and the young generation at large are plunged is too sad for such composure—but certainly we may regard it without a shadow of alarm. Human life and Christian society need Christ just as the earth needs the sun; and when men have satisfied themselves by experiment —they must satisfy themselves, they will not take our account of it; the theologians for the time have lost (and I fear righteously lost) the confidence of the great world —I say, when they have learnt by experiment in what debased and distorted forms the fair flowers and fruits of life unfold themselves in the cold dark shade of Atheism, they will be the first to bring them out into the living sunlight once more.

But this is the religious problem of our times—the reconciliation of humanity with the theology of the Church; and there will be much sore pain and bitter strife before it is solved. Now I reckon it the chief distinction of William Ellery Channing that he was one of the first to see with clear eye the disastrous tendencies of the dominant theology, and certainly one of the first to contend against it with a passionate earnestness which made him a kind of prophet in his times. His inmost soul revolted—and I touch here the centre of his theological system—in the space at my command I can deal only with central points—against that interior schism in the Divine nature, which the popular language of the dominant Evangelical school seemed to imply. The Son, representing mercy, acting on the Father, representing justice, by means of an infinite sacrifice of pain, and moving Him by the compensation of a costly atonement to let his mercy lighten on the world. That interior schism which the fundamental tenets of Calvinism seem to me to imply, presented to the world such a conception of the Divine nature and ways as rendered Unitarianism inevitable as a protest; and there, you will forgive me for saying, though you will not agree with me, I believe that its function ends. But thus far it was needed; and Channing gave voice to the protest with a fire, a depth of conviction, a persuasive eloquence, and I will add, with an Evangelical fervour—and this to me is Channing's chief charm among many noble and conspicuous qualities—which were unmatched in his generation, and almost in our own.

One thing he saw with marvellous clearness, and it is about the greatest thing in the universe to see, the unity of the Divine counsel, the Divine thought, the Divine love in the work of human redemption. From first to last it was in his sight the blessed and glorious work of the Divine Love. I should say that the key-thought of his theology was this deep sentence of St. Paul, "God was in Christ, reconciling the world unto himself." Not Christ reconciling God to the world, but God in Christ originating, carrying on, and completing, the work of the redemption of mankind. I should say that few Evangelical preachers have felt so deeply, certainly few have expressed so powerfully, the wealth of the attractive, regenerating, sanctifying power which the grace of God which is in Christ Jesus our Lord, supplied to the world. Here is the human as well as the Divine Gospel; a Gospel which will bear the full sunlight of man's reason, and will only reveal new depths of wisdom as well as love to explore. And if ever there is to be a reconciliation of the creeds of Christendom, if ever Trinitarian and Unitarian are to be gathered in the bosom of one Church, it must be on the basis of the unity of Father, Son, and Spirit in the redemption, the restoration, and the rule of the great human world. This gospel Channing proclaimed with a freshness and a convincing power which had their springs partly in the singular strength of his intellectual conviction, but mainly in the fervour of his spiritual life. He spoke with the force and the certainty of a prophet, and men listened to him as to one who was inspired. Channing saw full clearly, that if Christianity was the universal religion for man in all states, in all places, and for all time, it must include the whole field of man's legitimate interests and activities within its sphere. There was no human interest, there was nothing which promised any measure of benediction to mankind, which he did not connect by natural necessity with the Gospel. It is not enough to say that he was about the most eminent philanthropist of his time; a leader, and an early leader, in all those great movements which have added so much to the dignity of life and the happiness of mankind. About slavery, about drunkenness, about war, about education, about contact with and ministry to the poor, you will find him early in the century forecasting the line of Christian and social progress which, at the end of the century, we are following still with a rich harvest of blessing. He had to struggle hard, and at the cost of much personal suffering, to work into the mind and heart of Christians ideas and habits of action on social matters, which are now the familiar things of Christian wisdom and the daily paths of Christian love. He had wonderful insight, too, into the position and mission of England; and I think that one of the noblest passages in his writings is that in which he traces the service which England had rendered to humanity in her long, stern struggle with Napoleon, and deprecates and censures the newly-declared war. Many a noble passage, too, do his works contain on that course of public policy which maintains the strength and dignity of nations—that course from which we Englishmen have sadly wandered, but to which, thank God, we have now with full intelligence and steadfast purpose returned.

All this I might say and support by manifold and

striking extracts; but I made up my mind that there would be no space for extracts without infringing on time which will be employed to high purpose by others. So I must beg you to believe what many of you, no doubt, know perfectly well, that all which I advance I could support by ample quotations if I had time. But it is not enough to say this, it is only a part, and I venture to think the least part, of the truth. All his philanthropic work was the fruit of most sacred religious conviction. He was a philanthropist and reformer because he was a Christian, in days when such Christians were few; and this threw into his advocacy of those great measures of justice and mercy (the task of dilating on which is committed to other and more competent hands) a constraining and convincing power such as religious belief alone lends to the argument of progress. He threw himself with characteristic ardour into every movement which promised to forward the secular improvement of men and things around him, because he found it in his gospel; just as in an earlier age the "Yea, yea," and "Nay, nay," of George Fox and his Quakers in all their commercial transactions, first established the all-important commercial principle of fixed prices in retail trade. The book has yet to be written which shall show what society owes to religion in quickening and cherishing through their infancy the germs of all its most important reforms.

Another of the key-thoughts of Channing's religious system was the essential dignity of our human nature which had been systematically vilified—I can use no other words—by the dominant theological school. I have read in theological works of high repute statements about our human nature which equally dishonoured the wisdom which created it, and stultified the love which redeemed it. To Channing's eye, our nature, fallen, discrowned, dishevelled as it is, still bore sacred marks of the touch of the Divine finger, and was not dignified only but glorified by the Incarnation. Some of the very finest passages in his writings have for their text—I here quote his own words—"Human nature glorified in Jesus." In truth those large, spiritual, and most Christian ideas about man and God which the old Broad-Church party, of which the ever beloved and honoured Frederick Denison Maurice was the founder, developed, may be found writ large, early in the century, in Channing's discourses; while at the same time (and I believe that every great leader of a lasting progress combines two great streams of tendency) he combined with it the passionate fervour, the intense personal piety, the burning love to Christ, which finds utterance in Wesley's, Newton's, and Toplady's hymns, and which characterized the most evangelical of the Evangelical school.

And this leads me on, in closing, to the noblest and deepest source of Channing's influence on mankind—his life. There is much in his books, as we have seen, to account for his influence, though there is in his style a fertility of words and a reiteration of thoughts which is just a little wearisome to us in these days. But then we must remind ourselves that this new literature in his days was young, and young things are endowed with a copiousness and facility which are not without their uses, and which mature into felicity in time. And further, these great themes which occupied his pen, familiar now to us as daily bread and sunlight, had to be pressed by constant reiteration—" Line upon line, and precept upon precept," on the heart and conscience of mankind. Still there is a want in his style, though it is powerful and eloquent, of the subtle opalescent charm, that ἀνήριθμον γέλασμα which Æschylus saw on the ocean, and which plays over the pages of the great scholarly masters of style in the literature of the world. But then there was something larger and deeper than charm. There was a force there which mastered and compelled men. There was electric fire that set them in vital movement; there was the ring of intense personal conviction; there was the expression which none could miss, of a great, noble, self-sacrificing life.

And here I touch the chief point of all, and with this I close. A man's worth to the world after all depends on what he is, and not on what he says, or even what he does. The Life was the light of men, is the light of men, and will be to the end of time. What Channing was as a preacher and leader of progress is a great thing; the greatest was what he was in his own soul. If you want to know what he was as a preacher you must not only sit with the throng which gathered to hear his burning words, which hung upon his lips and listened breathless whilst Christ's ambassador pleaded as with Christ's own earnestness with human souls; you must follow him to his study; you must read his diary; you must catch the outbreathing of his inmost spirit to his Master; you must watch him breathing importunate prayer for the souls of men. I know not anything within the whole compass of theological literature more calculated than Dr. Channing's diary to impress young preachers with a solemn, almost an awful, sense of the sacredness of their vocation, and to cast them on the Master's grace in fulfilling it. "One thing I do," he could say, if ever man could say it, with an honest heart. And men observed him as a man whose whole being was consecrated to what he believed to be the greatest of missions, and who, if he preached Christ fervently from his pulpit, would have preached him as fervently from the rack and the stake, and would have gloried, like Paul, in being counted worthy to suffer loss and even death for his name. And beneath all this, the basis of it all, its strong unfailing support, was his inner fidelity, simplicity, and piety as a man. He lived to God; God was in all his thoughts; truly his fellowship was with the Father, and with the Son Jesus Christ. He felt, as few men have ever felt, the attraction of his Master's example; the inspiration of his Master's purpose; the constraining power of his Master's love. "The love of Christ constraineth me," expressed the inner secret of his life. And because he lived a Christian of a very noble and lofty type in the deep recesses of his own spirit, always aspiring after the Divine likeness and seeking ever fuller and yet fuller satisfaction in the contemplation of the Divine perfections and the communings of the Divine love, he was able to be as a beacon light in his generation to a great multitude, not in his own country only but throughout the world. It was given to him to work out for his own generation the path of a noble, lasting, and fruitful progress; and now that he is gone, "being dead he yet speaketh," he is speaking here to-night; yes, and the light of his life still flashes on far before us, and marks the line for our advancing steps. For himself, he has heard the word of the Master, "Go thou thy way until the end be; thou shalt rest and shalt stand in thy lot at the end of the days." And then few, I think, among earth's great ones will be crowned with more illustrious honour in the day "when the teachers shall shine as the brightness of the firmament, and those that turn many to righteousness as the stars for ever and ever."

The CHAIRMAN stated that Mr. Edmund Sturge had been asked to address the meeting on Dr. Channing's opposition to slavery. Though unable to attend, he had sent a letter, which would now be read:—

Mr. STURGE says: "There must be few who survive, who have any adequate conception of the tremendous social antagonism which Dr. Channing so boldly, nay, so cheerfully encountered, when, in his supreme allegiance to Eternal Right and Justice, he challenged the tenure of that vast iniquity which we have only seen demolished in our later years.

I had never the privilege of a personal acquaintance

with Dr. Channing; but, in the year 1840, my late brother, Joseph Sturge, undertook a mission to America, with the main object of attacking the apathy on this question, which then but too largely pervaded the Society of Friends in that country; in this he had the able and effective co-operation of John G. Whittier, and the work was blessed with no little success.

It was on his return that he gave such descriptions of Dr. Channing, and of those other "men of the time," and the warfare they were waging, as to place me almost as much " en rapport " with Dr. Channing, as though I had known him in the flesh.

Forty years have not effaced these impressions, and they impel me to add my feeble testimony to that of the gentlemen who meet to-morrow, that the "memory of the just is blessed."

MR. THOMAS HUGHES' ADDRESS.

Mr. Chairman and friends: The paper which I have been asked to read is entirely upon Channing as the anti-Slavery prophet. I feel it to be an honour to be allowed to take part in this festival, and to speak of Dr. Channing as one of that band of men and women, who, fifty years ago, made the cause of the slave their own in the United States, and in the face of rebuke and discouragement from society and the Churches, and of danger to life and property from the mob, persevered, through evil report and good report, until the victory was achieved, and the flag of the Great Republic, like our own, waved over none but freemen. I do not know how far you who are gathered here to-day in memory of a great and good man may agree with me; but to me it has long seemed that to that band belongs the highest place as benefactors of our race in this strange and eventful century—that the seeker for heroic and Christian lives, for the simplest, the truest, the bravest followers of the Son of Man—will have to turn to the Abolitionists of New England. I do not forget — I am proud always to remember—that Old England led the way, and that the struggle here, too, was one which tried men's hearts and reins. But honour to whom honour is due; and if we will try to think what our anti-slavery movement would have been had our eight hundred thousand slaves been scattered over the southern counties of England, instead of over islands thousands of miles away, and had belonged by law to the noblemen and squires in those counties more strictly than their rabbits and hares belong to them, we shall have little hesitation, I think, in yielding freely the foremost place to the group of New Englanders amongst whom Channing stood out a noteworthy figure —in some respects, undoubtedly the most noteworthy of all. Yes, as Mr. Lowell sings :—

> All honour and praise to the women and men
> Who spake out for the dumb and the down-trodden then—
> I need not to name them—already for each
> I see history preparing the stake and the niche,

> They were harsh, but shall you be so shocked at hard words
> Who have beaten your pruning hooks up into swords?
> Your calling them cut-throats and knaves all day long
> Don't prove that the use of hard language is wrong.
> You needn't look shy at your sisters and brothers,
> Who stabbed with sharp words for the freedom of others.
> No, a wreath, twine a wreath for the loyal and true,
> Who, for sake of the many dared stand with the few ;
> Not of blood-spattered laurel for enemies braved,
> But of broad peaceful oak-leaves for citizens saved.

This defence, which he who was to become one of their most powerful voices here finds himself driven to make for the Abolitionists, was never needed for Channing, and it is for this reason that I have referred to him as perhaps the most noteworthy of them all. For in all the excitement of a controversy which he felt to be for the life itself, and to be going down to the roots of things ; when the religious and respectable world shrank from the side of the teacher they had pretended to love and honour for thirty years ; when the finger of hatred and scorn was pointed at him in an all but unanimous press, as the fomenter of revolution and the associate of felons and fanatics—no word ever fell from his lips or pen which was not weighted with consideration for and sympathy with his enemies, and generous allowance for the difficulties of the Southern slave-owner. In his first great anti-slavery manifesto, his letter to H. Clay on the Annexation of Texas, he speaks of his own early residence in the South, and his life-long attachment to them thus : " There is something singularly captivating in the unbounded hospitality, the impulsive generosity, the carelessness for the future, the frank open manners, the buoyant spirit and courage, which marks the people," and from this he never swerved in later years when the contest had become envenomed. " Hitherto the Christian world has made very little progress in assailing and overcoming evil," was one of his sayings; and it was with scrupulous care that he strove to set some example of the divine method in the great controversy of his own time

Let me now, as briefly as possible, recall the position of the question in 1830. The struggle in England was drawing to an end. Those of you who are old enough will recollect those days, when children were brought up to use no sugar, and to give every penny they could call their own for the cause of the slave. How the time was one of bright hope and enthusiastic work, for the goal was full in view. On the 1st of August, 1834, the Act passed, and emancipation was a fact. In the United States it was far otherwise. There, year by year, the prospect was growing darker, and the clouds were gathering. The Southern tone had changed under the strain of the immense development of the cotton trade. Instead of lamenting slavery as an evil inheritance from their fathers, which was to be curtailed by every prudent method, and finally extinguished, Calhoun and the Southern leaders were now openly proclaiming it to be the true condition of the labourer, and the mainstay of Society. They were looking round eagerly for new slave states, to balance the steady increase of free states in the north, and by savage word and savage act were challenging, and trying to stamp out, every attempt to interfere with their domestic institution. Their challenge had been formally accepted, and the gauge of battle taken up in these very months. It was in this winter of 1830-1 that Garrison, the immortal journeyman printer, by extraordinary energy, got out the first number of the *Liberator*, declaring slavery to be a "league with death and covenant with hell," and pledging himself and his friends to war with it to the bitter end. Their watchword was, uncompromising, immediate emancipation. It was in this same winter that Channing went to spend some months at St. Croix. He had not been in a slave state since his boyhood, and he returned with all his old impressions confirmed and strengthened. Slavery he felt to be even a greater curse to the world than he had always proclaimed it. So he preached on his return to New England, and at the same time showed much interest in the work of Garrison and the uncompromising party, pleading for them that "deeply moved souls will speak strongly, and ought to speak so as to move and shake nations." No wonder that they turned eagerly to him in the hope that he would join them openly and lead their attack. But, for the moment, this could not be; the temper of the combatants, waxing fiercer day by day, was a barrier which he could not cross as yet; and no doubt the social ostracism—so formidable to one who had for a generation stood foremost amongst those whom his countrymen delighted to honour—weighed somewhat with him. He could defend the Abolitionists as "men moved by a passionate devotion to truth and freedom," which led them to speak "with an indignant energy which ought not to be measured by the standard of ordinary times," but join them at once he could not. And they, in their disappointment, were almost ready to denounce him as one of those recreant New Englanders who are addressed in the first stirring appeal in the Biglow papers.

> Wall, go along to help 'em stealin'
>   Bigger pens to cram with slaves;
> Help the men that's ollers dealing
>   Insults on your fathers' graves.
>
> Help the strong to grind the feeble,
>   Help the many agin the few;
> Help the men that call your people
>   White-washed slaves and peddlin' crew
>
> Hain't they sold your coloured seamen?
>   Hain't they made your envys wiz?
> Wut'll make ye act like freemen?
>   Wut'll get your dander riz?

The question whether Channing would have done well to have joined the Abolitionists at once will always remain fairly debatable, and will be settled by each of us according to the strength of his own fighting instinct. Those who blame him for delaying can, at any rate, call himself as a witness on their side. When at the end of 1834 the Rev. Samuel May, general agent of the Boston Anti-Slavery Society, in answer to Channing's expostulations as to the harshness and violence of their language, and the heat and one-sidedness of the Abolitionist meetings, turned upon him with, " Why, then, have you left the movement in young and inexperienced hands?

Why, Sir, have you not moved, why have you not spoken before?" Channing, after a pause, replied in his kindest tones, "Brother May, I acknowledge the justice of the reproof; I have been silent too long." Looking, however, at the man's age and character, I cannot myself join in casting blame on Channing. Other men might have deserved reproach for not emphasising their convictions in this way; but not he. At school he had gained the name of the Peacemaker. He had been true to that character for half a century. While a gleam of hope remained that the South might even yet move in the direction of abolition, a gentle firmness of remonstrance was the only weapon he could conscientiously sanction. And there was still such a gleam of hope in the lurid clouds. As late as 1832 the question of abolition had been discussed in the Virginian legislature. Some few of the best Southern public men still held the old doctrine, and were ready to work for gradual emancipation; they were actually doing so by a colonisation society, and other stopgaps, the hollowness and worthlessness of which had not yet been proved; the peacemaker might still hope to prevail. But now the time had indeed come when further hesitation would have left a stain on his armour.

I have said that the South were on the look-out for new territories into which to carry their slaves, and the devil rarely fails to find what they are in search of for men in that frame of mind. We must once more go back for a few years. In 1827 the Spanish American Colonies had gained their independence. Mexico, the chief of them, and the nearest neighbour to the United States, had from the first looked up to the Republic with hope and admiration. But from her great elder sister no response came. Her goodwill was coldly put aside, for she had declared freedom to all slaves in her borders, and these borders, unhappily for her, comprised a magnificent territory called Texas, as large as any four States of the Union, and eminently fitted for cotton growing, and, therefore, for slave labour. The temptation of this Naboth's vineyard soon proved too strong for the slave-holders, and an immigration of planters and slaves set in. The Mexican Government remonstrated, and high words ended in a declaration of independence by the new settlers, and fighting, which must soon have resulted in their defeat, for they scarcely amounted to 20,000 in all, but for the constant replenishment of their ranks by bands of filibusters from the other side of the Mississippi. By this means Texas maintained a precarious kind of independence, which she was endeavouring to convert into annexation to the Union. For some time every American statesman scouted so shameless a proposal; but by degrees the value of the country began to impress the Slave States more and more. Talk of "manifest destiny" began to be heard not only in the *New Orleans Picayune*, and in border ruffian meetings, but within the walls of Congress, till in 1835-6 it became clear that annexation, involving almost certain war with Mexico, was about to be submitted to the great Council of the nation. Here, then, was a new departure, involving on the part of the

F

nation a sanction of slavery such as had never yet been tolerated. Already Channing had begun to redeem his pledge. He had published a volume on slavery, taking firm ground against the furious madness of the Southerners, who were calling for the suppression of anti-slavery publications and setting prices on the heads of leading Abolitionists; and against the more odious respectable Northern mobs, which even in Boston had broken up meetings, and in New York had dragged Garrison through the streets with a halter round his neck, intent on hanging him. Channing had also opened his pulpit to May, the general agent of the anti-slavery societies. Now he stepped forward as a leader, and stood frankly side by side with the Abolitionists. Selecting for his correspondent Henry Clay, of Kentucky, the best and most moderate of Southern politicians, he addressed to him the most famous of his political writings, the letter on the annexation of Texas. I have already quoted from it one of many passages which showed his friendly temper towards the Southern slaveholders, but the most thoroughgoing Abolitionist could take no exception to the firmness of the position taken, or the power with which it was held. Time will only allow me to give the briefest outline of this masterly paper. "Congress,' Channing said, "is about to be called on to decide whether Texas shall be annexed to the Union. Public questions have not been those on which my work has been spent; but no one speaks, the danger presses, and I cannot be silent. There are crimes which in their magnitude have a touch of the sublime, and this will be one of them. The current excuses only make it more odious. The Annexationists talk of their zeal for freedom! What they really mean is their passion for unrighteous spoil. Of manifest destiny! Away with such vile sophistry. There can be no necessity for crime. Mexico came to us seven years ago—a sister republic just escaped from the yoke of an European tyranny, looking to us hopefully for good-will and sympathy. Instead of these, in our unholy greed we have sent them land speculators and ruffians who are waging war against a nation to which we owed protection against such assaults. Is the time never to come when the neighbourhood of a more powerful and civilized people will prove a blessing and not a curse to an inferior community? But the crime is aggravated by the real cause of it—the extension and perpetuation of the slave-trade, What will other nations, what, especially, will England say to it? We hope to prop up slavery by this filibustering; but the fall of slavery is as sure as the fall of your own Ohio to the sea. A nation provoking war by cupidity, by encroachment, and, above all, by efforts to spread slavery, is alike false to itself, to God, and to the human race. You are entering on a new and fatal path. Let the spread and perpetuation of slavery be once systematized and proposed as a Southern policy, and a new feeling will burst forth in the North. Let Texas be once annexed, and there can be no more peace for us. We may not see the catastrophe of the tragedy, the first scene of which we seem so ready to enact; we who are enlarging the borders of slavery, when all over Christendom there are signs of a growing elevation of the poor in every other country, we are sinking below the civilization of our day; we are inviting the scorn, indignation, and abhorrence of the world. In short, this proposed measure will exert a disastrous influence on the moral sentiments and principles of this country by sanctioning plunder, by inflaming cupidity, by encouraging lawless speculation, by bringing into the confederacy a community whose whole history and circumstances are adverse to moral order and wholesome restraint, by violating national faith, by proposing immoral and inhuman ends, by placing us, as a people, in opposition to the efforts of philanthrophy, and the advancing movements of the civilized world. Freedom is fighting her battle in the world with long enough odds against her already. Let us not give new chances to her foes."

I fear I can have hardly succeeded in giving you even a faint notion of the power of argument and beauty of style of this splendid protest. Occasions for speech now crowded on him thick and fast. In July, 1836, a mob sacked the office of the *Philanthropist* at Cincinnati, and drove Mr. Birney, its editor, from that city. Channing could not rest till he had written him the noble letter (published in his collected works under the title "The Abolitionists") exhorting him and his friends to hold fast the right of free discussion, but to exercise it as Christians. "The cross is the badge and standard of our religion. I honour all who bear it. I look with scorn on the selfish greatness of this world, and with pity upon the most gifted and prosperous in the struggle for office and power; but I look with reverence on the obscurest man who suffers for the right, who is true to a good but persecuted cause." But his complete identification with the Abolitionists did not come till the next year.

In November 1837, the office of the *Alton Observer* in Illinois was attacked, sacked, and its owner and editor, Lovejoy, the friend and fellow-worker of Garrison, killed while defending his property. New-England respectability was fairly startled at last. It was resolved by gentlemen of position, who had no dealings with Abolitionists, that a meeting must be held in Faneuil Hall, to protest against this and other acts of murderous violence, and to maintain the threatened right of free speech. A petition for the use of the hall was prepared, and the first signature was Channing's, over those of Sewall, Sturgis, and others of the best blood in Boston. The Board of Aldermen refused the hall; but the response from the whole Bay State to a temperate letter of Channing's in the *Daily Advertiser* soon convinced them that they had gone too far. The hall was granted, and the meeting held on December 8, and Channing proposed resolutions in favour of freedom of speech and meeting, prepared by himself. When these had been seconded, the Attorney-General of Massachusetts rose, and in a speech in which he likened the Alton mob to the fathers of the revolution, opposed the resolutions. The meeting wavered, and they would probably have been lost but for the speech of an unknown youth, who has since proved himself the greatest of anti-slavery orators, Mr. Wendell Phillips. The resolutions were carried in the end by acclamation, and for the moment the cause of freedom triumphed in Boston. But too soon the clouds gathered again, swiftly and ominously: and, from that time till his death, in 1842, Channing's soul was vexed, and his patience tried, by the blind fury and malignity with which the slave-owners' cause was pressed, and the frequent unwisdom and needless provocation with which the assault was met. Within a few days of the Faneuil Hall meeting, when a weak or vain man would have been glorying in his triumph, he addressed a letter to the *Liberator*, calling on the Abolitionists to show their disapproval of Lovejoy's use of force at Alton. "You are a growing party, burning with righteous zeal," he urged, "but you are distrusted and hated by a multitude of your fellow-citizens. Here are the seeds of deadly strife, conflicts, bloodshed. Show your forbearance now; your unwillingness to meet force by force; trust in the laws and the moral sympathy of the community; try the power of suffering for truth; the first Christians tried it amongst communities more ferocious than ours, and prevailed."

And now he himself had to bear bitter humiliation for the truth's sake, such as the refusal of the committee of his own Church to allow a service connected with the death of his friend Charles Follen, a leading Abolitionist. Yet he continued his work faithfully and even hopefully, speaking out at every dangerous turn in the conflict which was raging round him. His chief remaining works in connection with the slavery question are, "The Duty of the Free States," in which he defends the English Government for refusing to surrender a slave cargo who had overpowered the officers and crew, and had carried the brig *Creole* into Nassau: and "Emancipation," a tract on the great triumph in the West Indies. They are as thorough and able as the best of his works, and must be read by all who desire to know the length and breadth of his charity. As Englishmen, however, we may be allowed to refer with special pride to the last public utterance of his saint-like life. In the summer of 1842 he was dying slowly in the lovely Berkshire hills, when the return of August 1st, the anniversary of Emancipation in the West Indies, once more inspired him to lift up his voice for the outcast and the oppressed. To the men and women of Berkshire he spoke of the emancipation of the 800,000 British slaves begun eight, and finally completed four, years before. While giving full credit to the nation and the men who had been the instruments—"Christian men who had carried through their work against prejudice, custom, interest, opulence, pride, and civil power, against the whole weight of the commercial class thrown into the other scale"—he repeats once more, "Emancipation was the fruit of Christian principle acting on the mind and heart of a great people. The liberator of the slaves was Jesus Christ." And these are the last words he ever spoke in public, "The song 'On earth peace' will not always sound as fiction. Oh come, thou kingdom of God, for which we daily pray! Come, friend and Saviour of the race, who didst shed thy blood on the cross to reconcile man to man, and earth to heaven! Come, ye predicted ages of righteousness! Come, Almighty Father, and crown with thine omnipotence the humble strivings of thy children to subvert oppression and wrong, to spread light and freedom, peace and joy, the truth and spirit of thy Son, through the whole earth."

These were the last words of the great Christian leader of the New England Abolitionists. He died before his country had committed the great wrong the issues of which he had so clearly seen. The war with Mexico was declared in 1848, Texas and California were annexed, and, as Channing prophesied, all hope of peace between North and South, while slavery survived, vanished from that hour. Then followed twelve feverish years of futile compromise and smouldering civil war; the fugitive slave law, the free soil crusade in Kansas, the raid of John Brown at Harper's Ferry, culminating in secession and the extinction of slavery in the Union, in torrents of the best blood of the Republic, poured out at last like water to redeem that "strange new world" as the glorious inheritance of all men, without distinction of race, colour, or condition.

All honour to the brave and true souls who led the forlorn hope, and to him the wisest and greatest, and not the least firm, of all, whose memory we are met to day to keep green and fresh in men's minds. In thinking of his anti-slavery record, does not the lesson read somehow thus? There are times when it would seem that great causes in this mysterious battle-field of our race can only be upheld by an enthusiasm which can see but one side, backed by the strong arm prompt to return blow for blow. But such crises can only arise in human affairs from the failure of true insight, patience, charity, at some earlier stage of the drama. And, on the whole, we shall best serve God's purpose by bearing steadily in mind, that the victory of the Son of Man—which alone has made any and all other victories possible for his brethren—was won for our race by Him of whom it is said by the inspired seer, "He shall not cry, nor lift up, nor cause his voice to be heard in the streets; a bruised reed shall he not break, and the smoking flax shall he not quench; he shall bring forth judgment unto truth. He shall not fail nor be discouraged till he have set judgment in the earth, and the isles shall wait for his law."

THE DEAN OF WESTMINSTER'S ADDRESS.

When at Boston two years ago, I visited, in the beautiful cemetery of Mount Auburn overlooking the River Charles, the grave of William Channing. I read on his tomb the inscription which tells that "he was honoured not only by the Christian society of which for nearly forty years he was pastor, but throughout Christendom." This sentiment of universal respect was testified in

America on the day of his funeral by the mourning of all Boston, and the bells of the Roman Catholic chapel joined with those of church, chapel, and meeting-house of all Protestant communions, in tolling for the loss of one whom all esteemed and lamented. And this sentiment, irrespective of the peculiar opinions which he professed, or the peculiar sect to which he belonged, was not confined to his native country. With the exception of Jonathan Edwards in the peculiar branch of religious philosophy with which his name is identified, and of Dr. Robinson in the sphere of Biblical Geography, the fame of William Channing is, or at any rate was till very recently, the only splendour of American theology which had reached the Continent of Europe. It is not often that the great French Review, which for whatever reason bears the name of "the two worlds," condescends to notice any English speaking Divine. One of these few exceptions was in the thoughtful and brilliant article written by M. Charles de Remusat on the Life and Writings of Channing. And in Germany the most eminent of Catholic theologians, and certainly one of the best informed of all German writers on the condition of the various States and Churches of Christendom, the venerable and illustrious Döllinger, is reported to have said that with one exception Channing was the only theologian that the Americans had produced. What is it, we may ask, which justifies this widespread fame? What is it which justifies this celebration of the Centenary of Channing's birth on both sides of the Atlantic? First let me speak of the effect of his character. He was one of the rare instances, rare in all ages of mankind, of a man in whom was combined the dignity and moderation of a high ecclesiastic, or if we choose so to put it, of a calm philosopher, with a courageous enthusiasm on behalf of the more practical and popular objects of philanthropy. Such a union was to a certain extent seen in the career of Thomas Arnold in the Church of England, and Thomas Chalmers in the Church of Scotland; yet perhaps neither of these distinguished men, superior as they might be in other respects, presented so striking a contrast of qualities as was exhibited in the union of the sensitive, shrinking, cautious temperament, of which so many curious tales are rife even to this day in Boston, with the generous, outspoken expression of adherence to what was then in that city the unpopular and unattractive cause of the abolition of slavery. A character of this kind is doubly precious, because on the one hand it helps to justify in the eyes of ardent reformers of wilder, and so to speak, revolutionary tendencies, the value of that lofty unimpassioned vigour which belongs to the "edita doctrinâ sapientum templa serena," and on the other hand it tends to redeem the views of philanthropic zeal from the reproach which the recklessness and the folly of their adherents provoke from the more reasonable and moderate champions of light and sweetness. Secondly, he combined what is rare in any country, but perhaps most rare in his own, an unquestionable patriotism with a large comprehension and admiration of the glories of other countries. He loved with a passionate love the scenes of his early childhood, in the charming Town of Newport. "No spot on earth," he said, "helped to form me like that beach." It is indeed a curious reflection as we pass along that stretch of sands, and those projecting crags which overlook the vast roll of the Atlantic waters, that the same spot should have nourished two spirits so far asunder in their respective careers, yet so similar in their high aspirations, as Channing and our own Berkeley. What Boston, the intellectual centre of America, was to him, and what he as its intellectual leader was to Boston, it is needless to describe. But nevertheless he never surrendered himself to the besetting temptation which led so many of his countrymen to regard America as the only land of promise, the only sphere of moral and intellectual progress. No Frenchman, Catholic or Protestant, could have taken a more appreciative view of the character and writings of Fénélon than Channing in an Essay which he has devoted to the character and writings of the Archbishop of Cambray, and no Englishman could have been fired with a warmer zeal for the greatness and glory of Britain during the Napoleonic war than was this son of England's revolted children. The proof of this larger than any local or parochial sympathy is found in the fact that, not once only nor in one generation only, Channing's sermons have been preached in the pulpit of our metropolitan Cathedral, without affording the opportunity for a critical congregation to detect by any trace of provincial accent or thought, the source from whence they proceeded.

But, thirdly, this universality of his fame and of his sympathy, found its chief expression in the catholicity of his religious sentiments. Belonging as he did to the Unitarian communion, which at that time almost formed what we may call the established church of Boston, he yet rose far above it and beyond it, both in his particular expressions and in his general aspirations. "I value Unitarianism," he said "not as a perfect system, but as encouraging freedom of thought, and as breathing a mild and tolerant spirit into the members of the whole Christian body. I am little of a Unitarian. I stand aloof from all but those who strive and pray for a clearer light, who look for a purer and more effectual manifestation of Christian faith. I have little or no interest in Unitarianism as a sect." He strove, if we may use his own words, "to seize the true idea of Christ's character, to trace in His history the working of His soul, to comprehend the divinity of His spirit;" he strove "to rise above what was local, temporary and partial in that teaching to its universal, all comprehending truths." Without entering into any details for which this occasion would be unsuitable, it is sufficient to say that any one who deserves to exercise a permanent influence over the future, must breathe more or less of the spirit which animated this truly Christian philosopher. "He is a philosopher," said Coleridge, "in both possible senses of the word. He has the love of wisdom and the wisdom of love." Every one, of whatever Church, who identifies his teaching with the peculiar phrases in which, by ancient formularies, or modern party spirit, the temporary tendencies of this or that Church may have been expressed, clogs the upward and onward course of his words with an incumbrance which in after years will prove a serious obstacle to his reception on the roll of those whose works will live in every age and every country. Channing keenly felt the insufficiency, not only of the past but of the present. "Till a new thirst of truth," he said, "such as I fear is not now felt, takes possession of some gifted minds, we shall make but little progress. The true Reformation is yet to come; the time is, perhaps, at hand when all our present sects will live only in history. Could I see before I die but a small gathering of men, penetrated with reverence for humanity and the spirit of freedom, and with faith in a more Christian constitution of Society I should be content." It is this appreciation of a fuller truth than he had himself attained, which places him in that succession of gifted men whose thoughts form the golden thread of Christian Theology. Origen, Clement of Alexandria, in their better and more lucid moods, Chrysostom and Augustin; Erasmus in the sixteenth century; Falkland, Tillotson, Henry More and Whichcote in the seventeenth; the serener atmosphere and freer thoughts which formed the background of the philosophic mind of Butler, the vigorous common sense of Paley, and the generous enthusiasm of Wesley in the eighteenth century; Arnold, Frederick Robertson, and Dean Milman in the nineteenth century—to speak only of the dead and not of the living;—it is among these that Channing will take his place as having contributed, in no mean degree, towards the right appreciation of the right proportions of faith, towards fixing the attention of Christendom on the ideal, the moral, the spiritual, which is also, and for that reason, the truly divine, the truly permanent, the truly supernatural, element of Christianity.

DR. W. B. CARPENTER'S ADDRESS.

At this late hour of the evening I shall confine myself to a very few words to express my heartiest accordance with all that has been said in regard to the worth and the vast influence of the great man whose centenary we are here met to commemorate. And let me begin with two little anecdotes which will show the extent of that influence. As long ago as the year 1827, while I was staying with my father at Newport in the Isle of Wight (being then little more than a boy) he became acquainted, through the introduction of a friend, with the minister of the Independent chapel in that town. Channing's Essay upon Milton had then recently reached this country; and my father found that young minister in a state of the highest excitement, reading the essay while walking up and down his study. His spirit was stirred within him; he said that he could not sit still while he read it. The earnest utterances of that Essay on behalf of freedom of thought and speech, which were not surpassed by Jeremy Taylor or by Milton himself, stirred the mind of this young minister; and I will now tell you who he was—Thomas Binney. You all know what an important influence Thomas Binney, who removed to London two years afterwards, exercised in that great movement of thought, which (as I am sure that my friend Mr. Baldwin Brown agrees with me in thinking) has completely altered the aspect of the theology of the Congregational body.

Another little anecdote refers to a very recent time. I take a very great interest in the advance of free thought in the various sections of the great Scottish Presbyterian Church; and early association has led me to keep up communication with many of its leaders. In correspondence with a friend last year, I learned that even in the straitest sect of Scottish Calvinism there is an opinion held that Channing and Martineau must be subjects of the "uncovenanted mercies" of God. They, of course, restrict to themselves the "covenanted" mercies; but they feel that such men *must* come within the recognition of that great Being who looks upon all alike.

You are all aware that some of his earliest published writings were protests against the then dominant Calvinism of the New England Churches; and in refreshing my remembrance of these, I have been extremely struck with finding how entirely his view of the baneful influence of that system (consistently carried out) on the human mind, is applicable to the philosophy now fashionable among many of those who claim to be regarded as advanced thinkers. He considered it "one of the greatest of all errors to attempt to exalt God by making Him the sole cause, the sole agent in the universe, by denying to the creature freedom of will and moral power, by making man a mere recipient and transmitter of a foreign impulse. This, if followed out consistently, destroys all moral connection between God and his creatures. In aiming to strengthen the physical, it ruptures the moral bond which holds them together. To extinguish the free will is to strike the conscience with death, for both have one and the same life. It destroys responsibility. It puts out the light of the universe; it makes the universe a machine. It freezes the fountain of our moral feelings, of all generous affection and lofty aspirations." Now, only substitute "matter" for "God," and you will find that Channing's appeal to that noblest part of our nature, which is the distinctive prerogative of Man, is as true against the doctrine of Human Automatism, as it is against the Calvinism which I have heard appealed to as its backer.

Now I am asked to say some words with reference to Channing's advocacy of all movements relating to the elevation of the human race. His recognition of the dignity of human nature has been so ably dealt with this evening, that I need not say a word more on that topic; but I would point out that it was this recognition which made him feel most acutely the evil of sin, and dominated every utterance that he gave on the means of averting it. He was constantly appealing to first principles—those first principles which find a response in our intellectual nature, in our love of truth,—in our moral nature, in our sense of right; and every word that he uttered in this advocacy was to encourage endeavour for what he termed the elevation of the soul. And what he defined as elevation of soul was (1) Force of thought exerted for the acquisition of truth; (2) Force of pure, generous feeling, not merely the entertaining these feelings, but the earnestness with which they were felt; and (3) Force of moral purpose in action, that purpose which is cultivated by the habitual sense of effort which he speaks of as most contributing to moral growth. Man (he says) owes his growth, his energy, chiefly to the strife of the will, that conflict with difficulty which we call effort; and in those noble utterances of his with regard to liberty, he shows how many restraints tend to the truest liberty, how man by struggling against these restraints elevates his own powers and becomes the victor, and how every restraint that does not foster that tendency to liberty is evil, while every restraint that does is good.

There is one part of his grand Essay on Spiritual Freedom which seems to me worthy to be compared with the Beatitudes of the Sermon on the Mount; where, after saying that "to be free is to withstand the influences which menace the intellect and heart," he goes on and shows, in a succession of pithy and vigorous utterances, how every part of our nature is to be freed by effort. In that grand Essay, Sir, there is one passage that impressed me, on reading it recently, with the force of prophetic insight; that passage in which he adverts to the duty of Governments. He asks, How is the Government to serve the cause of spiritual freedom in promoting energy and elevation of moral purpose? "Not (he says) by teaching or persuasion, for that is not its function; but by action, that is, by rigidly conforming itself in all its measures to the moral or Christian law, by the most public and solemn manifestations of reverence for right, for justice, for the general weal, for the principles of virtue!" "In its relations to other governments it should invariably adhere to the principles of justice and philanthropy; by its moderation, sincerity, uprightness, and pacific spirit towards foreign states, by abstaining from secret arts and unfair advantages, by cultivating free and mutually beneficial intercourse, it should cherish among its citizens the ennobling consciousness of belonging to the human family, and of having a common interest with the whole human race." Then he says, "As it is the first duty of a statesman to build up the moral energy of a people, he who weakens it inflicts an injury which no talent can repair; nor should any splendour of circumstances, or any momentary success, avert for him the infamy which he has earned. Let public men fear nothing so much as to sap the moral convictions of a people by unrighteous legislation, or a selfish policy. Let them put faith in virtue as the strength of nations. Let them not be disheartened by temporary ill-success in upright exertion."

Now, since those words were written, what have *we* seen as the verification of them? We have seen the downfall of the Slave power in the United States; we have seen a nation rising in its might, in response to the appeals of its noblest men, and destroying that Slave power

What happened in a neighbouring Kingdom? We have seen a man raising himself by a combination of circumstances—with great ability of his own, no doubt—to the supreme power, becoming the ally of England, and for a time the trusted friend of our Sovereign and her Consort; and we have seen that man alienating by secret arts, by underhand measures, for his own aggrandisement and the aggrandisement of his nation (as he believed), the friends he once possessed, and exciting that universal suspicion in every country in Europe, which led to his downfall. I need not further point the moral; many of you will perhaps think with me, that it is even now finding an illustration nearer home.

Only one word more in reference to Channing's advocacy of the Temperance cause, because that is as pregnant an instance as I could produce of the value of his appeal to first principles. Channing distinctly states that the great evil of intemperance is the enslavement of the man who gives way to it. All other evils, in his mind, are subordinate to this. He is glad that the dreadful nature of this vice should make itself apparent in the evil it produces; but he says it is in the vice itself that the greatest evil exists. Now, Sir, these are words which appeal to our deepest convictions, and at the same time to our noblest feelings; and I look upon Channing as the one who, more than any other in modern times, brought all social questions to the test of the highest principles, and who, in laying down those principles, did not merely formularize them as part of a moral code, but appealed to our own moral sense, and our own love of truth and right, and our own love of humanity and of all that is highest and best in humanity to give them effect. And I may conclude by a reference to one whose name is known to all of you, and whom I think I may here name without egotism—Mary Carpenter. I would say that it was entirely in the spirit of Channing's utterances that she worked. She had faith in human nature; she had faith that there was a holy spot in every child's heart that could be touched; and she had a faith in God, who would help and guide her in all her attempts at the elevation of those, whom the crimes (as she considered) of society had degraded from the high position to which human nature is capable of being exalted.

DR. R. LAIRD COLLIER'S ADDRESS.

Mr. President and Friends: This Centennial anniversary of the birth of Channing should mark, not so much the close, as the opening of an era. It should not be so much a commemoration as a consecration, for if it should only be an hour of vain hero-worship—a worship Channing never gave and could not accept—it were more fittingly rendered to the name of conqueror or warrior, and not this friend of the people, of publicans and sinners, this man of sorrows, with whose stripes we are healed. Not one of the principles to which Channing's whole genius and endeavours were consecrated has taken deep root in the hearts of the people or been enacted in the customs of Christendom. Religious equality: The subordination of Christian dogma to Christian charity, in Channing's understanding of it, nowhere, in an organized way, finds acceptance. Religious opinion, and even superstition, is on all hands subsidized. Social equality: The subordination of all artificial and extraneous human distinctions to the welfare of the lowest and lowliest of the race is only the dream of the visionary, it is not so much as the vision of the dreamer. War is still waged, not only upon the strong, but upon the weak, without either provocation or explanation. The peoples are oppressed by this strain and stress upon resources at home, and the youth and courage of our races are sacrificed to the ambition and folly of politics and politicians. The thrones of Europe are still propped upon the points of bayonets. And man, the pride of Channing's intellect, and the passion of Channing's heart, is still starving in the hovel, still agonizing in the death of battle, still swinging by the neck on the gallows by society's approval or indifference, still staring upon society from behind prison gratings —a perpetual process of the unwitting wickedness of criminal legislation. A century since Channing was born! Since then steam speeds around, and electricity girdles the earth. Forty years since Channing died! Since then mechanical contrivances, physical facilities, and luxurious civilization have made enormous progress. But man, the rapture of Channing's religion, and the fascination of Channing's philanthropy, is still under the heel of the hero and monarch. Then, I repeat, this should not only be a feast of Commemoration, but the rather a pentecost of Consecration.

The principles that Channing preached from his pulpit, proclaimed from the platform, and published in his pamphlets, were in his time, as in our time, to the spiritual mind almost axiomatical. Now, as then, to "the wise and the prudent" they are not practicable. I do not mean, of course, when I speak of Channing's principles, many of his casual speculations either in theology or philosophy, for Channing was not primarily a theologian, but a mystic; not supremely a philosopher, but a poet. That he would have been a Congregationalist, and not an Episcopalian, in his views of Church polity; that he would have been a Unitarian, and not a Trinitarian, in his conception of God, we could have foretold from the necessity under which he was placed to weigh and consider these matters by the times in which he lived, and the controversies then active in his community. So honest was he in head and heart; so fearless was he in speech and with pen; so independent of social fawning or worldly emolument; so intuitive was it with him that the ignored and despised cause was God's contention in the earth; I say we might have foretold that he would have been of that company of men and women of all lands and all times, who have kindled fires of agitation here and there, the world over, which have eventually burnt up sacred superstitions and venerable wickednesses;—men and women, for the most part, whose triumphal cars have been hailed and saluted centuries after they were dead and gone, but who in their own time were prophets standing in the market-places with outstretched arms, crying unto the people all the day long, who only passed by to scoff and deride. But I repeat, Channing's life did not go forth and fill the earth with controversies about creeds of only dogmatic and speculative value. He said of himself he was no more wedded to his own opinions than to the opinions of other men. Were he the same personality living in our midst to-day, in his religion and in his philosophy he must still be a mystic and a poet. And in this there is no assurance that he would be either a Congregationalist in Church government, or a Unitarian in theological opinion; but there is, if I may so say, the sign of God written on the soul of an honest man, that with the growth of human society, he would not be less than these, but larger than these!

Coleridge said of Channing, after a personal interview with him:—"He subordinated the true to the good without encroachment on the worth of either," and that "he had the love of wisdom and the wisdom of love." The Rationalist in religion stops short in "the love of wisdom," and so is chilled by doubt, and is palsied by speculations. He is, therefore, both sceptical and superstitious. He dwells only in the lower hemisphere of the mind where thought is the schoolmaster leading to the faith or sight of the soul. Channing was no Rationalist, settling all questions of heaven and earth by the square and plumb-line of the mechanic.

His abode was in the upper hemisphere of the soul, whose faith or sight he could neither gauge nor measure. His last words uttered on earth were these: "I have received many messages from the Spirit;" and as he received them he went forth and delivered them. A mystic and a poet understands these words, but give them to a Rationalist and he analyses them, and he finds Channing made a mistake, for there is no evidence that there is any such Spirit, and so these messages which the dying Channing reported he had received from the Spirit were only subjective psychical phenomena, and no messages at all. Channing dates precisely the time of his spiritual change of heart, which in after-life he said was so great a change it ought to be called the New-Birth. The mystic and the poet understands all this world of reality, but the Rationalist "has not so much as heard if there be a Holy Ghost." The Rationalist is the dreamer, the mystic and the poet is the doer.

The great work which Channing did in his day was that of applying intellectual theories to social institutions. His clear estimate of the original dignity and immortal worth of man was made concrete in the schools, the libraries, the churches, in the education of the masses; the social elevation of the ignorant, the poor, the vicious, and the criminal. This mystic, this poet, was possessed by principles which could not always be made genial and harmonious by formal logic.

But, I repeat, Channing was no esoteric dreamer, but a practical preacher of righteousness. This man, who claimed liberty of thought and speech as his Christian birthright, laboured also in season and out of season according to the measure of his strength, to propagate views of God's character, and of man as the child of God; of man's duty on the Earth, and of his immortal life after death, which were beneficent as well as rational, ennobling as well as true.

He knew of no other law in religion than that which he observed in the physical world, of cause and effect, and that if in the spiritual world we are to reap the fruits of liberal religion we must sow the seeds of liberal religion. He held it to be the Supreme, if not the sole value of liberal Christianity that " it was suited to reconcile men's hearts to God, to purify and exalt human nature, to advance charity and philanthropy and all the peculiar virtues of the gospel." He says,— " Did I not believe this, I should say, let us lay down the weapons of controversy, for even if we hold the truth it is not worth contending for . . . . it is only a theorem for the speculative intellect, an abstract science without power to operate on the character, inapplicable to the conscience and life. Again I say, it is the *practical influence* of *liberal views* which summons us to the *zealous advocacy* of rational and consistent Christianity."

He deplored the religious chill that seemed to settle upon the faith and to dampen the zeal of the Rationalists of his day, and said: " It is best then to acknowledge with Christian frankness and sincerity that men of liberal minds have often been defective in fervour; that the spirit of free inquiry has sometimes, if not frequently, an indifference about opinions; and that the dread of bigotry and fanaticism has hurried many into the opposite extreme of langour and insensibility." . . . and then adds, "The affections are not useless parts of our nature. . . . the affections give to the character its principal charm and interest. Is affection an improper tribute to be offered to God? . . . It is of great importance that religion should be an affection of the heart, as well as a conviction of the understanding, because it is to govern in a soul which is agitated by various passions, which is powerfully solicited by the mind, and which is prone to contract a sensual taint and sordid character. These strong and dangerous propensities of human nature are not to be counteracted by mere speculations of the intellect. The heart must be engaged on the side of God and duty."

The God of Channing's heart had not only a name to live while He was dead! There are men who tell us they have no God; very well, we understand them. But there are others who have a God but seem to have no need of Him. He is, according to their telling, both deaf and dumb. He neither hears their cry nor answers it. To the soul of Channing God was a "living God"—personal, fatherly, friendly, with whom he held most loving and closest communion and converse. On the Mount of Transfiguration came the glory to his countenance and the glow to his speech. God did make his face to shine and his lips to speak. He touched every subject and thought with the emotions of spiritual love, so that controversy was grace in his hands, and polemics were lifted into a devotion.

But all Channing's philosophy, philanthropy, and religion had their roots in his divine perception of the original dignity and inherent worth of man. No writer before his time had this clear understanding of Christ's revelation of the immortal value of a human soul! Man as man, not hero or saint, simple or gentle, wise or base; but man in hovel, in hospital, in prison; man as God's own child, Christ's own brother, Heaven's own heir! So in society or in religion; all that degraded man in theory or custom he sought by every Christian means to remove from the paths of man's ennobling and progress. He espoused every view of God, man, duty, society, destiny, that he deemed pure and elevating and Christ-like!

First of all, Channing was a preacher. A Unitarian minister in Boston. I do not mean to say his theology was yours or mine, but it was the theology, not only of his intellect, but of his heart. And he believed and said that Unitarian theology was meant, in his opinion, not only to enlarge the spiritual vision, but to stimulate the fervour of the heart. And when I say he was a preacher, I mean that he was a preacher by temperament. He was a preacher like Savonarola, like Chrysostom, like Wesley, like Chalmers, with a burning agonizing love for men. He was a man of deep feeling. He was an intuitional man. In speaking of a friend, he said: " He is one of the intuitive men whom I take delight in much more than in the merely logical." He was a converted man—a man of deep religious insight and experience. He was a trained speaker. His university course fitted him for this, and he cultivated speech and writing. His style in both was almost perfect. He was a writer, and used the magazines and journals of his day, to which he had access, and published sermons, and addresses, then pamphlets on education, social and political questions; then volumes of sermons and addresses. Then his correspondence was very large, and his letters were treatises.

But I have not yet touched the source and secret of his power and influence. It was not supreme genius; I do not rank Channing as of the first order of intellectual genius. He had great symmetry of mind. It was not profound scholarship. When he graduated at the university his technical education would have been inadequate for his matriculation at Harvard now. He had very little theological training. In that day of great preachers—Dewey, Gannett, Greenwood, Buckminster, the Wares, the Peabodys—they got their power and inspiration from living men. They began their ministry young, before they were moulded into mere scholars— whilst there were yet picturesqueness, enthusiasm, courage, playing freely in their hearts and hopes. They learned the business of their profession like lawyers and doctors. He tells us, that during his college career two or three evenings a week he attended Debating or other literary societies, and here he trained himself to speak. When he began his ministry he had already learned to read and to speak with accuracy and felicity. He had not the advantage of imposing physique. or of generous health. He was an invalid from the time he began his mission to the close of his illustrious life. And yet this man rose to be the prophet of his century!

Then I am yet to tell you in one word the spring and secret of his power—Love! His soul was aglow with love. He had on earth what we only hope for in heaven—perfect love. He went to God through love. God was perfect love. He went to Christ through love, for Christ was perfect love. He went to heaven through love, for heaven was perfect love. He lives in the hearts of the race through love, for his heart was perfect love. *He realized* the reality of love. It was love that broke down all barriers in religion. He was the friend of religious equality—not tolerance, but equality for Atheist as well as Pietist. It broke down all class and artificial distinctions. He said, "I am a leveller," and wrote to a friend in England: "Aristocracy and a true humanity are irreconcileable. There may be much kindness toward the lower orders, but no respect for them as men—as essentially equal by the participation of God's image. Humanity they cannot have."

In beginning this address I said this day should mark not the close of an era but the opening of an era in the life of Channing. And I meant this: He is still alive. But the century since his birth has been powerless to enact, if not helpless to comprehend, his gospel of the dignity of man. We still leave man in the meshes of ignorance, the bitterness of intolerance, the unrestraint of intemperance, the chains of slavery, and the cruel savagery of devastating and desolating war. Then let this Commemoration Feast be also a Consecration Pentecost. We claim to be in sympathy with the principles and views to which Channing consecrated his life. It is in reverence for these that we have come together. Would we could catch the fervour of his mind, the glow of his heart, the glory of his deeds! Then we should cease our dreaming and our vain and useless speculations, and go forth to rekindle the fires of love with an ennobling and rational Christianity. This is the Feast of Commemoration that we should celebrate! Let not the hour end till it has been born into our hearts and purposes to go forth and plead with the servile and selfish men of our generation, as he pleaded with the sordid and sinful men of his generation to work the works of God, that liberty may speed to the ends of the earth and peace to all its nations; that simple truth and Christian charity may be the sole emulation of children of the same family, until we all come to "owe no man anything, but to love one another." America has raised up illustrious names, statesmen, scholars, philanthropists, divines—Washington, Lincoln, Emerson, Garrison, Channing; but the greatest of these is Channing! Some had faith, and some had hope, but Channing had charity, "and the greatest of these is charity."

The Rev. W. DORLING: Ladies and gentlemen, I was to have spoken just before Dr. Carpenter addressed you, but I preferred saying to your Secretary that I thought there were gentlemen who had greater claims upon your attention than I have, and at this late hour I shall not attempt to make a speech. All I meant to say about Dr. Channing—and I had not a little to say which I am sure would have come out of my own heart—I shall omit, and content myself with simply moving the resolution which has been placed in my hands: "That the hearty thanks of this meeting be given to the speakers this evening in cordial sympathy with the deep admiration they have expressed for Dr. Channing's life and work, and in the trust that the spirit of his teaching may ever more and mere prevail in the practical religion of the future."

The Rev. H. IERSON: The Chairman will, perhaps, kindly allow me to second this resolution in order that I may be able to say just one word—that the Rev. Wm. H. Channing would certainly have been with us to-night—his daughter we have had the pleasure of welcoming—but that he is engaged in laying the foundation-stone of the Channing Memorial Church in Newport, Rhode Island. There ought to be one practical result out of this centenary besides the cheap edition of Channing's Works which you will find at the doors. They want money for this church in Newport, and if any of you are desirous of contributing towards the building, I shall be happy to transmit any subscriptions that you may be pleased to place in my hands.

The Resolution was carried with acclamation.

The Rev. P. H. WICKSTEED: Before we separate I will move a vote of thanks to the Chairman. There is no man whom we should have been more pleased to see in the chair on this occasion, or who has worked harder or more faithfully for the cause in which Channing was interested.

Professor C. B. UPTON seconded the motion, which was cordially agreed to.

The CHAIRMAN: I am much obliged for the kindness with which you have received the very poor efforts that I have been able to offer you to-day. It is a great honour to me to have held office on such an occasion, and I hope we have all felt benefited and encouraged by the good words we have heard. I know of no way more calculated to extend and popularize the knowledge of the Christianity and beautiful religiousness of Channing than to circulate to the utmost in our power the works that are now, by the spirited efforts of one gentleman, placed before you at such a very low price. I think we cannot do better than purchase as many as we can and give them away. I again thank you for your kindness.

The meeting was closed with the Hallelujah Chorus from Handel's Messiah on the organ.

THE BELFAST MEETING.

On Wednesday, April 7th, at three o'clock, a large number of the Unitarians of the Belfast and the surrounding districts commemorated, at a collation in the Music Hall, the centenary of the birth of Dr. William Ellery Channing. Amongst those present were :—Hon. W. Porter, General Richmond, U.S. Consul; Messrs. E. J. Harland, J.P.; John Miller, J. P. (Comber); W. J. C. Allen, J.P.; John Campbell, G. W. Wolff, James Dickson, John Carlisle, N. Oakman, H. Darbishire, J. R. Neill, R. W. Gordon, G. Fisher, Joseph Mackay, A. Hunter, H. Murray, Marcus J. Ward, John Rogers, R. M'Calmont, W. Spackman, John Little, Wallace Boyle, J. W. Russell, G. K. Smith, F. Frankfort Moore, J. Salvage, John Smyth, junr. (Banbridge); W Smith (Banbridge); Revs. C. J. M'Alester (Holywood); J. Hall (Ballyclare); English Crooks (Ballyclare); Hugh Moore, M.A. (Newtownards); Harold Rylett (Moneyrea); David Thompson (Dromore); Barnard Gisby (Rademon); David Thompson (Hopeton Street); J. J. Wright (Mountpottinger); Thomas Dunkerley, B.A. (Comber); James Kennedy (Larne); T. H. M. Scott, M.A. (Dunmurry); R. J. Orr, M.A.; James Cooper, H. T. Basford

(Banbridge); Joseph Pollard, James C. Street and A. Gordon.

In the absence of Dr. Ritchie, J. P., from illness, James M. Darbishire, Esq., took the chair.

Rev. A. GORDON stated that letters of sympathy with the object of the meeting, and regretting inability to attend, had been received from Revs. R. Campbell (Templepatrick), President of the Non-subscribing Association, and Moderator of the Remonstrant Synod; S. C. Nelson, M.A. (Downpatrick); David Gordon (Downpatrick); Robert Cleland, B.A. (Crumlin); John M'Caw (Killinchy); Wm. Whitelegge (Cork); W. S. Smith (Antrim); J. Miskimmin (Greyabbey); W. Napier (Clough); John Jellie (Cairncastle); Messrs. J. R. Musgrave, J.P., High Sheriff of Donegal; John Millar, J.P. (Lisburn); W. Robertson (Belfast); Thomas Andrews (Comber); Professor Hodges, M.D. (Belfast); Messrs. Edward Gardner, LL.B. (Downpatrick); T. M'Clelland (Belfast); and David C. Patterson (Holyrood). He would read the following extract from the letter of their venerable friend Rev. S. C. Nelson, which would explain the cause of many absences :—

" Our county election is unfortunately fixed for Wednesday next, 7th inst., and it will therefore be impossible for me or any from this neighbourhood and from many other polling districts of County Down, to attend the Centennial. I should have rejoiced to move the excellent resolution assigned to me. We owe a great debt of gratitude to Mr. Spears for his many unwearying and useful labours, and to him and those who have co-operated with him for this crowning and magnificent undertaking of 100,000 copies of Channing's whole works at a price which brings them home to every family, however poor. From experience of more than half a century, I can testify to the welcome accorded to Channing's writings among all denominations. In 1825 I gave a copy to Dr. Laurin (then my brother Bishop of Dromore), of the first sermon of Channing's then published in England, delivered, I think, at the ordination of Jared Sparks. He expressed a wish that some of the ordination sermons preached by clergymen of his diocese were as good, and added that, but for scholastic terms and metaphysical definitions, we might all be more in harmony. He used to boast of being descended from the Huguenots, the promoters of liberty, industry, improvement, and progress, both on the continent and in these countries. More recently, a talented and truly Catholic priest of this neighbourhood, to whom I gave a copy of our former cheap edition, thanked me cordially for what he called one of the most agreeable, instructive, and useful presents he had ever received. I have also found Channing's works on the library shelves of numerous Methodist ministers and laymen, as well as many of our so-called 'orthodox' Presbyterian brethren. Trusting that your meeting may not only be a present success, but an omen and promoter of closer harmony and unity among ourselves, I am, yours sincerely,

"S. C. NELSON."

The CHAIRMAN desired to thank the meeting for the honour they had conferred upon him in asking him to take the place of Dr. Ritchie. They all knew that Dr. Ritchie's spirit was with them though he was absent in the flesh. He must confess that it was very gratifying to him to preside over such a representative and influential meeting of Unitarians, whose hearts and souls were united that day with those of hundreds of others in that land and in America, gathered together to do honour to the name and memory of one of the greatest men whom God ever blessed the world with. They knew that in all parts of the world the name of Channing was revered and honoured. Few men had done so much to spread the broad and liberal views of Unitarianism, and few men had acted so nobly in the cause of religion as William Ellery Channing. Therefore it must be a great gratification to them to see the 7th day of April, 1780, commemorated that day, and it was a day that would be in their remembrance as long as they lived. It would be fulsome on his part to eulogize Dr. Channing. His writings, speeches, and lectures were known to every one present, and he was sure that there was no lady or gentleman, no boy or girl, who ever took up Dr. Channing's works, or read any of his discourses, that was not wiser and better for having done so.

Rev. J. C: STREET moved the following resolution :—
"That, in commemorating to-day the one hundredth birthday of William Ellery Channing, we desire to pay a reverent tribute to the transcendent beauty and sweet-

ness of his character, which shone through all his acts and all his writings, and constitutes for all time a living exemplification of manly dignity and Christian worth." He said that, not there alone, but in many other parts of the English-speaking world, citizens were gathered together to do honour to the name and to the works of William Ellery Channing. There were possibly others than those of their spiritual communion, who were being brought together on that day, and who in other parts of the world were doing as they were doing, and were united with them in a common bond, and making them feel that they were engaged in a genuine work. A hundred years had passed since the advent of William Ellery Channing to the world. Many men had lived and died within that period, but of the many comparatively few were remembered as Channing was remembered that day. Generations rose and passed away, and only the souls that were richer and riper and rarer in the race were perpetuated in the memory of those who succeeded them, and it was because there was something exceptional in the character and work of Channing that men and women were assembled that day to honour his name. For his own part he did not look upon Channing as one of the greatest of men, but he looked upon him as one of the best of men. He was not profound in his scholarship; he was not majestic in his mental powers; but there was, nevertheless, a wealth of scholarship, and there were powers of singular sweetness which belonged to him, which had secured for him a place which men of larger scholarship were never able to occupy. Whatever scholarship and mental power he had, they were hallowed and sweetened by one of the kindest, gentlest, and most loving spirits that ever radiated in the heart and brain of a human being. One of the main characteristics of Dr. Channing was the perfume of sweetness and holiness, and high-toned morality, which were to be found running through all he said, and all he did, and which would for ever remain as his greatest monument among mankind. He thought the resolution he had read would embody not simply the sentiments of that meeting, but of all those whom they represented in the North of Ireland, and it would also effectually embody the sentiments of those who in different parts of the world were that day commemorating the birth of Channing. The resolution recognized the wonderful sweetness and beauty of Channing's character, and no reader of his writings could help being impressed with that. Channing had to hold aloft a banner that required firm hands to support it, and throughout all his controversies, and they were many, and all the battles in which he engaged, and they were not few, his greatest foes admitted the wonderful sweetness of his thoughts and utterances. Dr. Channing dignified controversy and exalted reasoning. He made those who disputed with him feel that the battle was not a battle of persons nor a battle merely of opinions, but a battle of earnest principles to which men were to look carefully and reverently in order that they might find what was the truth. Men who entered into a controversy in that spirit, though they might not convince their opponents, yet by their tenderness of manner and sweetness of method they could not help winning for themselves a profound love and reverent respect. Among all the controversial writings which had sprung from the bosom of their Church, none had such a wide distribution as the writings of Channing. He seemed to be the fitting instrument of the moment. There was a great transition in public opinion and religious thought at the time that Channing stepped forward to enter upon his life-work. He seemed a man peculiarly adapted to addressing himself to the controversies of the age. He carried on his part of the controversy in such a way that those who came after him, having their work well begun, had now almost brought it to a successful issue. Dr. Channing was, as the chairman had told them, a Unitarian. He was Unitarian with very pronounced and definite views. He differed very much from many of his brethren who were round about him, and his views were not in harmony with many of those held by his brethren to-day. But, while that was the case, he was a large-minded man who could put himself in his brother's place, and sometimes see with his brother's eye, and feel with his brother's heart. He knew that there were points of view different from his own, and that it might be that an opponent saw some large measure of the truth of God. Hence he was largely tolerant in his spirit; and hence, though he was born in a sectarian Church, he rose out of it, and entered into the universal Church of God with all its sympathies for mankind; and hence on that day they had all over the English-speaking lands men of broad views in their free Church who were banded together to do honour to the name of Channing. They did not care so much for the precise form of his thought or whether it expressed exactly their form or not. What they were honouring that day was the large, tolerant, catholic spirit which looked out into the universe of God, and sought for the brotherhood of humanity all over the world. In all probability, in the history of the world Channing would be remembered more for the work he did in connection with great social questions than even for his work in connection with theology. For, after all, he dared say they all felt theology was a changing topic, that it shifted its aspects as the world became larger and as the truth of God became more and more revealed; but the great principles of morality and freedom and righteousness, which belonged to all Churches and to humanity, remained with them perennially, and would be to them a source of perennial strength. Dr. Channing threw himself as few men did into the great living controversies of the day. He was always pleading for righteousness and the great principles of human freedom. Channing was a man of weak physical constitution, but he seemed to have mastered himself, and to have held himself supreme in the tabernacle of his own nature. He belonged to a class of men who gave an exaltation to their common humanity. He was one of the men they prized as representing the highest type of personal character. In the ordinary forms of daily life; in the ministrations among his people; in the utterances from the pulpit;

in his sympathies with the slave; in his work amongst poor sufferers from drunkenness, he carried with him a spirit of wonderful consecration, which tended to remove many a stain from human life. It was that which prominently distinguished him, and made him a power and inspiration wherever he went, quickening the men and women about him, and elevating them into closer relationship with the spirit of the Living God. They that day bore their humble testimony to the worth of that great life, and, forgetting many things, they joined hands, as they might not have done for many years, in a reverent recollection of one who, representing none of their differences, symbolized their living unity.

Mr. JOHN CAMPBELL, in responding to the call to second the motion, rejoiced to have an opportunity of commemorating the birthday of Dr. Channing. They might establish memorial churches and might publish and circulate Dr. Channing's works, but they would do most honour to his memory by humbly endeavouring to catch his spirit and imitate his virtues.

The CHAIRMAN proposed the following resolution:—
"That, in celebrating Dr. Channing's special services to our own denomination, we would thankfully recognize that breadth of soul and delicacy of spiritual touch which have rendered his expositions of Christianity the common property of liberal minds in all Churches."
He cordially agreed with every word in that resolution. Every one who endeavoured to imitate Channing's

virtues would be wiser and better, and able to do more good in his own way. It was a very important thing that in their libraries they should have such cheap editions of Channing's works, and that even the humblest cottage could be provided with them. Dr. Channing was one who undertook the duty of improving mankind, with a delicacy of refinement peculiar to himself. He had the power of attracting the young and the old, and of inspiring them with his own simple spirit. He was a hater of intemperance, and, in short, he was a reformer in every sense of the word, and everything that he did was done with sincerity and moderation. He did not believe that Dr. Channing ever made an enemy, though he took part in various religious discussions. He was tolerant to a degree, though firm in his own opinions. Any one who read his writings would see what a simple and pure-minded man he was; that he was never seeking his own welfare but rather that of every one connected with him, and he had, therefore, left a name behind him which would immortalise him. He (the chairman) thought that one of Dr. Channing's most beautiful books was *The Perfect Life*. In that work he exemplifies the life he led himself.

Rev. ALEXANDER GORDON, in seconding the resolution, said: The April sun is shining on our festivity, in happy unison with the pure and radiant spirit of him whose birth we are met to commemorate, whose virtues we remember, and whose services we gladly and proudly own. Channing belongs to a class of influential minds always rare, and differing in some important respects from the majority of those who have influenced the course of thought, and decided the temper of theology in the various denominations and Churches. There are those of whom we can hardly think, apart from the peculiar ecclesiastical position in which they found themselves placed. It would be impossible, for example, to consider Aquinas except as a schoolman, Hooker save as an Anglican, Bossuet in any other light than that of a Roman Catholic, Jonathan Edwards except as a Calvinist, or John Relly Beard save as a Unitarian. Noble as these men were in their thoughts, and sympathetic in their hearts, nevertheless if they were stripped of their specific theological ideas, and taken away from their recognized ecclesiastical position, with the loss of their mental vesture, their identity would be destroyed, they would become unrecognizable units in the crowd. On the other hand, there are those whose precise theological or ecclesiastical place seems to be rather the result of what we may call the accident of time, birth or training, than the effect of any uncontrollable innate tendency. Such men as Tauler, the Dominican; as Valdés, who though we look upon him as one of our own predecessors, lived and died in the Roman Catholic Church; as Henry Scougal, the Scottish Episcopalian; as Bishop Berkeley, or Dr. Doddridge—such men as these belong not to one Church, but to all. Remove them from their immediate surroundings, and one might transplant them into almost any other Christian community, and the thoughts which they would breathe, and in the main the words that they would speak, would awaken the self-same echoes which they had awakened before. Now, to neither of these classes does Channing properly belong. We cannot escape the plain duty of classing him as a denominationalist. He was one of those men of whom Baxter was the grandest example in the seventeenth century. Baxter was the typical English Nonconformist; we might even call him the creator of our Nonconformity. It was the unresting eagerness and vehemence of his conscientious scruples, rejecting any, even the least, obedience to an outer law as distinguished from the inward spirit, which gave definition and courage and permanence to those mighty spiritual forces which have moulded the history of English Dissent. And yet, though Baxter was a denominationalist, and the founder of denominationalism, Presbyterians have long ago forgiven his telling them that Presbyterian was, to his ear, an "odious name;" Unitarians are perfectly content that he should assure them that the creed of Athanasius, to his mind, interpreted best the deepest of all mysteries, the mystery of the Divine Being; even Conformists gathered round his monument the other day at Kidderminster, acknowledging that the spirit of catholic charity lived in the man, and was by no means diminished or injured by the strength of his Nonconformity. I think we may say this likewise of Dr. Channing, and perhaps in a larger degree. Dr. Channing was decisively a Unitarian. We may describe him as the creator of modern Unitarianism. For he it was who, when he took up the Unitarian name, first succeeded in attaching to that theological designation its modern significance and present power. That name which our forerunners in the great age of the Reformation knew not; that name which Servetus never heard, and which Socinus rejected; that name which survived in obscurity, cherished by a picturesque community nestling among the Eastern hills, far away beyond the woods and thickets which fringe the vast arid plain of Hungary; that name which was revived in England by the learned Bidle and the pious Emlyn, but the use of which died with the men; that name which was borne aloft once more by the gentle heroism of Theophilus Lindsey, and made by him synonymous with a rigid Scriptural Monotheism, and a complacent doctrine of philosophic necessity; that name, when Channing took it up, acquired a new application, and a spiritual importance which it never had attained before. The famous sermon at Baltimore, in 1819, first told Unitarians what their name really meant or might mean. Here in Ireland, I believe, the actual use of the name Unitarian dates from Channing's time and influence; and in Ireland the name has always been conceived in Channing's sense. It was not always so interpreted in England. To understand what Channing's services to us as a Unitarian denomination have been, we must realize what he has made our name distinctively import. That which Priestley thought impossible, and, if possible, inexpedient—the amalgamation under one name of the older Arian and the rising Humanitarian party—was seen, under the influence of Channing's teaching, to be not only feasible, but inevitable. It was made so by the unique strength of Channing's affirmations, by the self-surrender of his tolerant spirit, by the power with which he put forward the moral as well as the spiritual ground of our faith, by the fidelity with which he showed that, while our metaphysical differences may be many, there are points of union which bear witness to a common Christianity in all. It was this great doctrine of a common Christianity, preached by him in season, and some thought, out of season, which enabled him to be so commanding and elevating an influence, not only in the little church of which he was the mainstay and vindicator, but also, and scarcely less, amongst enlightened minds of all other Churches. We cannot say that Dr. Channing's work proved a bulwark in defence of the citadel of Christianity, such as was presented by the labours of the erudite Lardner or the industrious Norton; we cannot claim for him the frank philosophic acumen of Priestley; we cannot say that he has compelled the intellect of Christendom to reconsider any cardinal dogma in the same way as Socinus has done with regard to the dogma of the atonement. But this we can say, that in all the Churches around he has made men feel that there was something grander and better, something nobler and truer, than either what they had been fighting for or fighting against. He has made men feel that Unitarianism, as he preached it, must be interpreted as a witness, lofty and peerless, for spiritual freedom, for evangelical charity, for the religion of Christ Jesus undefiled. So it has happened that now, a hundred years after his birth, we find, in the nations round about, and in the Churches, whether orthodox or heterodox, men rising up to pay a tribute of reverent homage to the works and services, to the true and Christian spirit, of William Ellery Channing. We know that in Italy, this very day, in the capital of the most invincibly orthodox type of Christianity, a little band of noble spirits, with the Senator Mamiani at their head, are assembled to bear witness to the emancipating power of Channing. We find the same movement as far off as the northern snows of Iceland. We find it wherever the English language is read, and Channing's works in their original form are accessible. We find also, that these works have been honoured in translations, to an extent to which no other works have been honoured, except the Bible and the Pilgrim's Progress. Last month there happened in the city of Buda-Pest a very interesting ceremony. It was a wedding between the son of the Lord Lieutenant Daniel, one of the leading names in our own Transylvanian Church, and a Roman Catholic lady. The ceremony was performed within the chief church of the Reformed or Calvinistic body, lent for the occasion, and the officiating minister was our own Bishop Ferencz. Amongst the crowded congregation who witnessed the unwonted spectacle, was that noble specimen of a true Christian gentleman, Bishop Török, the Calvinistic Bishop of Buda-Pest. When I received this very morning the news of that remarkable incident, it struck me as possessing some features of an augury. Here was the marriage of Unitarian truth and Catholic piety, solemnized amid the not unmoved or unsympathetic presence of the Calvinistic community. This was the very work of Channing. It was not merely a proclamation of divine truth, it was the wedding of this with a charity not less divine, and the effectuation of the union in noble forms of social righteousness. As we contemplate the influence and power of such a life, we may take courage and renew hope. Thinking over what our great ones have done in the past, we may go forward, in the strength of God, to vindicate the spiritual kingdom of His Son, in the days that are present and that shall be.

The resolution was passed unanimously.

JOHN ROGERS, Esq., moved the next resolution :— "That, in recording our sense of Dr. Channing's ceaseless exertions through the pulpit and the Press, in the cause of freedom, culture, and philanthropy, we rejoice to witness the continual spread of principles of which he was the intrepid and enthusiastic advocate." The labours of Dr. Channing in the cause of religion were taking effect in his country, and they had only to read the newspaper to see that those principles were making way amongst the people. The great influence which Dr. Channing's works had on the minds of men was proved by the fact that those works were translated into many languages.

General RICHMOND, United States Consul, said he would not follow the eloquent example of those who had

I

preceded him, but should merely take advantage of the opportunity of expressing his full sympathy with the objects of this meeting. He sympathized with it from the bottom of his heart; and well he might, for he came from a place where the memory of Channing was present as a living virtue. In that part of America the places which he visited, and in which he spoke and worked, were in a historic sense classical. His writings would continue to exercise their influence over the people. His memory is fresh and green with the great assemblies of men and women who were that day united with them in celebrating the anniversary of his birth. He was glad to pay a tribute to the memory of one who did not belong to any one sect, or any one country, or any one age. Without feeling in accord with all his religious opinions, he rejoiced to be present that day to take part in the proceedings.

The Rev. C. J. M'ALESTER moved the fourth resolution: "That we commend the public spirit which has achieved the issue of a Centennial shilling edition of Channing's works, and regard the welcome accorded to his writings in both hemispheres, as a happy omen of the progressive influence of high thoughts, fitly embodied in a captivating literary form." He said, he had great pleasure in taking part in this centennial celebration. Those who had preceded him had dwelt on the character and writings of him to whom on this interesting and impressive occasion our thoughts are turned in admiration and gratitude, and they had spoken in just terms of his pure and holy life, his eloquent expositions and vindications of Christian truth, and his noble utterances in the cause of freedom and humanity; but they have represented him as not having been distinguished by great intellect or by profound scholarship. It may be so; but it is something better than great mental powers, or vast scientific knowledge, that has won for him so high a distinction: it is his spirituality of character. With intellectual powers of no mean order and with scholarship not to be despised, he combined a holy and sainted life, and spiritual endowments, which raised him high above his fellow men, and won for him the admiration of the wise and good. And now, when a century has been completed since his birth, and in many places, on both sides of the Atlantic, the occasion is being suitably commemorated, I am sure that thousands acknowledge the obligations which they owe to him, both for mental culture and for spiritual strength. For myself, I feel that I am largely indebted to Dr. Channing for helping me at that critical period when, just preparing to enter on the work of life, the opinions are so often unsettled; and on the one side a spirit of doubt and unbelief attracts, and on the other superstition seeks to enslave. At that time it was my good fortune to meet with those remarkable essays, one on the character of Napoleon Bonaparte, another on the life and writings of John Milton, and a third on the character of Fénélon, which excited my admiration by the glowing and eloquent language in which they were written, and still more by the noble, generous, and Christian sentiments which they contained. Soon after, a friend put into my hands the famous Baltimore sermon—I believe the first publication of Dr. Channing which was circulated here—and I was deeply impressed with the simple yet profound exposition which it presented of Christian doctrine. I soon after read his Discourses on the Evidences of Christianity; and as from time to time his other discourses and addresses appeared, I sought them with eagerness, and always read them with pleasure and advantage. It is not, I suppose, much more than half a century since in this country attention was first drawn to Dr. Channing's writings; and since that time what a mighty influence they have exercised! Far beyond the limits of a denomination that influence has spread, and it has largely tended to promote broader and more liberal views in various Churches. He only who rules the nations of the world, and raises up from time to time wise and good men to instruct and guide the people knows how much Channing's own country owes to the exhortations, the pleadings, and the warnings which he poured forth against war, and intemperance, and slavery, and in behalf of God and the dignity of the human being; in behalf of Christ and his Gospel; and how much his teachings contributed to awaken the public mind, and prepare them at length, albeit through the horrors of a civil war, to escape from that evil which so long weighed down the energies and dimmed the glory of a great nation.

By the bold and enterprising effort of one man, the Rev. Robert Spears, and the liberality of those who have encouraged and aided him to carry it out, 100,000 copies of the Centenary edition of Channing's works—the only complete edition, I believe, yet published—are now being issued from the press, the price *one shilling;* and thus they will be brought within the reach of all, and may find their way to the humblest workshop and the poorest cabin ; and we may believe that so long as the English tongue continues to be a living language, the writings of Channing will be prized for the Christian sentiments which they contain, and the elevating views which they inculcate of God and humanity. For our own land we may safely say that, in proportion as our statesmen and legislators, our scholars and divines, learn the lessons which Channing so earnestly inculcates ; lessons drawn, we believe, directly from the word and spirit of the Gospel ; lessons of the evil of war, the folly of ambition, and the enslaving power of sin; and in proportion as they are guided by the principles of justice, mercy, and peace, for which he pleads, we shall grow, not perhaps in extended territory, but in prosperity, in goodness, and in the respect of other nations. And should the time come in the distant future when, under that mysterious law which seems to govern the rise and glory, the decline and fall of nations, kingdoms now mighty shall be brought low, and other lands shall in the history of the world take their place, even then must the writings of Channing be treasured among the richest relics of our sacred literature and the most enlightened expositions of divine truth.

E. A. FUHR, Esq., seconded the motion, which passed unanimously.

The proceedings concluded with the usual vote of thanks to the chairman.

THE ABERDEEN MEETING.

(*From the Aberdeen Free Press.*)

A PUBLIC Meeting was held, on April 5th, in Blackfriars Street Hall, Aberdeen, to commemorate the hundredth anniversary of the birth of Dr. William Ellery Channing. There was a large attendance, the hall being well filled, and the Rev. G. T. Walters, George Street Unitarian Church, occupied the chair.

The CHAIRMAN, in introducing the proceedings, intimated that the Rev. Edward Lang (Dee Street Methodist Free Church), who had intended to be a speaker on this occasion, was unavoidably absent, and he also stated that the invitations were not given to the speakers, nor were they supposed to be accepted, on any ground of doctrinal agreement, but on the ground of religious sympathy of a broad and liberal kind.

Mrs. CAROLINE A. SOULE, President of the American Woman's Universalist Association, gave an address on "The Spirit of Channing's Life." She said the name and fame of Channing had been familiar to her from her childhood, as they were to the children of all intelligent American families, for however much people might differ on the other side of the sea in regard to the correctness of Channing's theology, they were united as to the solemn beauty of his life. One and all were proud of their countryman; they loved him as a man, they admired him as a writer, they respected him as a religious teacher, and they cherished his memory as that of one who never failed, in the hour when Truth sounded her bugle-notes, to come to the front and bear her banner into the very thickest of the conflict.

To catch thoroughly the spirit of Channing's life, they must remember the circumstances of his birth. Born, as he was, while the war of the Revolution was in its travail, and of patriotic parents, it was easy to see that his spiritual inheritance was an indomitable love of freedom, and an equally strong hatred of all that was enslaving. The boy who had seen his father entertain at his own table George Washington, the father of his country, could scarcely have other than that spirit which would fight its way from all trammels, secular or religious, and rise up as on eagle's wings to the clear sky of victory —victory over all that was false or little or low, all that was unworthy of a child of God. The spirit of that life whose birth they now commemorated was broad, bold, brave, bounteous, benevolent, and beautiful; and if they read his life carefully, they would not be able to find a single page on which they could not mark the one or the other of these.

Besides remarking the circumstances of his birth, to catch thoroughly his spirit they must remember that his parents were both individuals of rare natural gifts. Channing, though comparatively poor at birth in this world's goods, had yet a grand inheritance—gold that could not be stolen, jewels that could not be lost. Inheriting from his parents a character that was spotless, and from his country one that was noble, they might say, without irreverence, he inherited a portion of the kingdom of God—which was, inward righteousness, peace, and joy. The predominating qualities of Channing's life might be seen in his boyhood and early life.

In his maturer years, he was singularly free from bigotry and prejudice, was an ardent yet consistent advocate of religious liberty; broad in his own views, he still would not force them upon any one, believing that it was the right of every individual to exercise his own faculties in the investigation of religious truth. He abhorred a sectarian spirit; he laboured not so much to build up *a* church as *the* Church—the Church of Christ; not to develop the truth of a sect, but the truth of God. Yet, when the time came for him to reveal his convictions on any point of theological inquiry, he was bold and brave, yet ever magnanimous—rejecting decidedly those views which seemed to him erroneous, but never believing that error was guilt. He made a distinction, also, between an opponent and an opponent's views. The latter, if they seemed wrong, he was bound in honour as an apostle of truth to contradict and to discuss; yet he was courteous and gentle to the man in error.

Channing was a free giver in his thoughts, and also a free giver in material things. The beauty of his spirit was seen in his generosity to his opponents, in his sympathy with the suffering, in his tenderness to the sinful, and in his self-consecration to what he conceived to be the duties of a Christian minister. His ideal was high; perhaps the world has not seen one higher.

Rev. JOSEPH VICKERY (Blackfriars Street Congregational Church) gave an address on "Channing as a Social Reformer." He said it was the great merit of Channing, born on the eve of that great French Revolution which was to shake all nations, that he was among the first to catch the new spirit of freedom and inquiry, and to apply it to the consideration of practical questions. In his very youth he caught all the ardour and patriotic aspiration of that new period, and the glow of it never died away from his face. Channing's position in regard to all questions of social reform and progress is best expressed by the emphasis which he constantly laid upon the action of the individual. He had a distrust, which was perhaps too great, in the mere machinery of philanthropy, and he was perhaps somewhat disposed to under-rate the action of wise governing policies upon the condition of society. And yet it is impossible, in the reading of his speeches, his letters, and his various sermons, not to perceive that he had clearly recognized and firmly grasped the one principle which, more than all other principles, lies at the heart of social progress. Reformation must begin from within, and in this respect Channing's ideas of social reform are pre-eminently Christian.

But it was not less characteristic of Channing's attitude to society as a reformer, that in all his ideas, his aim was constructive rather than destructive. He recognized in the ascendency of every institution, however evil or objectionable in certain of its features, the outcome of the conflicting motives of a complex society. The true policy of reform is to see, not how much we can cut away, but how much we can save. To understand the social questions which confront us, we must trace them to their origin. Not only by temperament but by conviction, Channing was opposed to all indiscriminating attacks upon the evils and errors of society. He knew both the danger and the error of uncritical reform. His social radicalism was deep and fervent, but it was a radicalism which took a wide survey of the conditions of human life, and made large allowance for the infirmities and ignorance of men. In the firmness, yet moderation and breadth, with which he held and expressed his principles, in his clear recognition of the real difficulties at the root of our social troubles and disorders, in his healthy and genuinely Christian trust in the inherent goodness of human nature, in his preference for a moral and religious policy, rather than for what is purely political and mechanical, Channing was admirable. I join in the praise of Channing this evening, because he was not only an illustrious member of the society of Christ and God, but because throughout his spotless career he was entirely faithful to that policy of progress which he believed to be the only one which is supremely true and divine.

The CHAIRMAN spoke on "Channing's Influence on the Future of Humanity," and said that Thomas Carlyle had given us the hero as divinity, as prophet, and as priest, but not the hero as a saint. Amid the struggles, the hopes and fears, of mortal men there was room for a type of heroism such as that. If by the word "saint" they might mean one who sought to purify the world from its sin and shame, and to make life glorious by truth, devotion, and love, then William Ellery Channing might stand, for them, the hero as a saint! And how did such men influence the world? They did not cause a great and sudden commotion. They did not shake the pillars of an empire. Their influence was of a gentler kind, rather to be compared to the subtle breath of spring, which calls forth flowers and grass to make joyful the dark, sad, wintry soil.

With reference to Channing's influence upon the religious future of Humanity, Mr. Walters said that he believed that many had been delivered from a hard, selfish dogmatism, and prejudices had been removed. Channing was a Unitarian; and people who had been trained, as he himself had been, to regard that word with the utmost horror, found, when reading Channing's works, that a Unitarian might be a sincerely pious and good man, might be a Christian in that very highest sense of the term, which means Christ-like. Things could not remain as they were. People were beginning to ask why theological differences should divide men of earnestness and faith, why the great cause of civilization and progress should be checked by reason of jealousy or suspicion between various men who, whatever their doctrinal differences might be, were striving to win the world to a nobler and purer life. In the future, then, the Churches of Christendom would realise that there was something more truly precious than creeds and formularies; that the distinctions of sect were but mean and paltry in the sight of Him who gathered to his side the beggar and the outcast, and who enunciated, in the surprised hearing of a Samaritan woman, his grandest principle of religious faith, that the true worshipper should worship the Father in spirit and in truth. The influence of Channing would also save many from drifting away into the extremes of Materialism and Atheism. This service would not be less than the other. Over the stormy seas of controversy; whilst the waves of sectarian passion roll and break; while theories of extreme partisans dash in vain tumult and perpetual babble, the light of Channing's faith will shine as from the lighthouse top, will calmly assert, through the dark and stormy night, the perpetual and unfailing love of God; and, from age to age, many a human soul, struggling through life, shall be guided to the harbour where every sorrow and every pain shall be hushed in the eternal peace.

The thanks of the meeting having been heartily given to the speakers and the Chairman, the proceedings were closed by the Rev. Joseph Vickery pronouncing the Benediction.

THE TAVISTOCK MEETING.

(*From the local paper.*)

On Wednesday evening the Unitarian body of this town celebrated the Centenary of Dr. William Ellery Channing, the great American philanthropist. After the tea, the company adjourned to the Guildhall, where a public meeting was held.

The Rev. T. L. BADCOCK presided, and observed that they had met to commemorate the advent of one of the brightest and noblest spirits that America had produced. Not only was William Ellery Channing great in philanthropic work, but he was a highly spiritually minded man. The Chairman alluded to the popularity of Channing's works, and stated that through the liberality of the British Unitarian Association 30,000 copies had been published, and had resulted to a great extent in the widening of thought among men who were being trained for the ministry in various Christian bodies. Mr. Badcock then called on the Rev. W. Sharman, of Plymouth, to give a sketch of Dr. Channing's life.

The Rev. W. SHARMAN said they were assembled to celebrate the hundredth anniversary of the birth in Rhode Island, Newport, of William Ellery Channing, a man whose name to-day commanded the reverent admiration not only of the sect which his connection made illustrious, but of the catholic religious world. That night the late president of the Congregational Union and the Dean of Westminster would offer their tribute to the memory of this great man. Longfellow had long ago laid his wreath of verse on his tomb. No American since Washington had left such an influence for good. Dr. Channing came of a good and wholesome stock. On the father's side there was Devonshire blood, the Channings having gone over in the time of the *Mayflower's* expedition, from Newton Abbott. His mother's side—the family of Ellery—were a race of ardent patriotic Americans, and the name of the grandfather was attached to the Declaration of Independence. The boy was born into wholesome circumstances among a community consisting chiefly of working men, all of whom believed that the one great duty a parent owed to a child was to give him a good education. Channing was a bright, generous, healthy boy, brave both physically and mentally. He was very observant, and while quite young learnt a great deal from the discourses of Dr. Styles, of Philadelphia. After a brief college career Channing determined to make choice of the ministry. He acted as private teacher and schoolmaster at Richmond for two years, but there he so neglected the laws of health in the pursuit of study that he contracted a weakness of constitution which never left him. In 1800, when twenty years of age, he returned to Newport, his father having died, and rendered what assistance he could to the family. He continued his studies, and went under a course of strict self-discipline. He was afflicted with an irritation of temper, probably the result of ill-health, and determined to cool it and subdue it to the law of right, declaring that he would never enter on the work of the ministry until he had brought it into subjection. In his twenty-third year he was called to the Federal Street Congregational Society at Boston, and whilst occupied in the round of ministerial work he took a deep interest in philanthropy. His protest against the war which America entered into with England was one of the noblest specimens of moral bravery that had ever been recorded in America. About the year 1815, the stricter Calvinists made an attack on their more liberal brethren, and a controversy ensued in which Channing took a very active part. Although a great defender of Unitarianism, yet he said of himself, only two or three years before he died, " I am but little of a Unitarian, have little sympathy with the system of Priestley and Belsham, and stand aloof from all but those who strive and pray for clearer light." To the end of his life he felt enthusiasm for everything that was progressive; he was always fond of freedom, but always on the lines of Christian evolution. In 1830, owing to a failure of health, Channing had to take refuge at Santa Cruz, where he saw slavery in its worst forms. He was convinced, however, that while its physical evils were greatly exaggerated by the Abolitionists, its moral evils surpassed description. On his return to Boston he determined to take an active part in the anti-slavery movement. Mr. Sharman then described Channing's anti-slavery crusade, and the dauntless spirit he maintained in the steady pursuit of his purpose, notwithstanding the opposition he encountered from every quarter.

The meeting having thanked the lecturer for his admirable address, a similar compliment was paid to the chairman, and to the ladies who had presided at the tea tables.

THE MANCHESTER MEETING.

On Wednesday evening, April 14th, a soirée and public meeting was held in the New Town Hall, Albert Square, under the auspices of the Manchester District Unitarian Association, to celebrate the birth of Dr. Channing. There was a very large gathering. On the evening previous near one thousand tickets had been sold. There was a most brilliant assembly. The Mayor's magnificent suite of rooms was thrown open for the accommodation of our friends. Tea and coffee having been served in the tea-room, an organ recital of pieces from Sir R. Stewart, Macfarren, and Rossini's was given by Mr. J. Kendrick Pyne There were present among others—Alderman C. S. Grundy, ex-Mayor of Manchester, who occupied the chair, the Rev. Chas. T. Poynting, B.A., and Mr. John Dendy, junior, joint Secretaries of the Association; the Revs. Chas. Wicksteed, B.A., Wm. Gaskell, M.A., James Black, M.A., Joseph Freeston, P. M. Higginson, M.A., T. Lloyd Jones, W. M. Ainsworth, J. T. Marriott, C. C. Coe,

D. Walmsley, B.A., Noah Green, S. A. Steinthal, J. B. Lloyd, Benjamin Walker, Richard Pilcher, B.A., J. Harrop, Wm. Mitchell, Silas Farrington, E. W. Hopkinson, John Moore, James Harwood, B.A., John McDowell, George Ride, F. H. Jones, B.A., J. K. Smith, W. Mellor, H. Thomas, W. C. Squier, J. Perry, B.A., J. G. Slater, W. G. Cadman; Messrs. E. H. Greg (Styal), Smith Golland, G. W. R. Wood, treasurer of the District Association, Robert Nicholson, Henry Leigh, E. Winser, Jesse Pilcher, E. C. Harding, J. Barrow (Bolton), J. Barrow (Styal), John Heys, John Dendy, John Thomas, Richard Wade, H. J. Leppoc, Z. Smith, Henry Coffey, O. Oldham, Alex. Ireland, Archibald Winterbottom, W. H. Herford, B.A., H. Long, T. H. Baker, F. Holland, F. Monks (Warrington), Councillor H. Bailey, W. Horrocks, W. H. Talbot (Deputy Town Clerk), J. Bellhouse, James D. Oliver, Richard Peacock, Thos. Swanwick, Thomas Rawson, and Colonel Shaw (U.S.A. Consul), J. H. Nicholson, John Reynolds, John Barrow, Prof. Roscoe, F.R.S., and Dr. John Watts.

THE CHAIRMAN (Alderman C. S. Grundy) spoke as follows :—It is one of the privileges accorded to laymen to be invited to preside on occasions like the present; but if I felt that the acceptance of the position necessarily involved a complete development of our subject, you will readily conceive that I should have shrunk from the task. Knowing, however, that my deficiencies will be supplied by one whom I shall shortly have the pleasure of calling upon, I have the less hesitation in standing here, even in this public place, and offering, from a lay point of view, a few introductory observations in acknowledgment of the obligations we are under to the eminent divine in whose honour we are assembled. We are here to pay our homage to the memory of William Ellery Channing. It is not the habit of Unitarians to idolize individuals. Acknowledging, as we do, that One is our Master, even Christ, we are at all times sensitive lest we should unduly exalt any other name, and thereby impair our loyalty to Him. In this respect we differ from many of our fellow Christians, and thus avoid those causes of division which arise from declaring that we are of Paul, or Apollos, or Loyola, or Calvin, or Luther, or Wesley. Whilst acknowledging the great virtues of those religious leaders, and respecting the convictions of all who have felt constrained to follow them, we, as a branch of the Christian Church, have ever felt that no secondary personal name is wide enough to cover the field of our religious discipleship. Nay, so jealous are we of our individual freedom that most of us disclaim all written definitions and creeds; and, from the fear of being brought under intellectual thraldom, some amongst us go so far as to refuse even the impersonal description of "Unitarian." If, however, we picture to our minds an imaginary roll of names representing broadly the various divisions of the Christian faith, and that upon that roll it became necessary to inscribe one as a representative of the views commonly held by Unitarians, there is perhaps none that would command so many suffrages as that of Channing. Two or three generations ago that name would probably have been Priestley or Belsham. Those honoured men were, however, but the pioneers of the doctrinal restoration; the forerunners of modern Unitarianism. The almost universal prevalence in their day of what is called orthodoxy compelled them to be controversial, and forced them into what, when viewed from a more recent standpoint, appears a combative or destructive attitude. Whether the work to which they and their immediate successors devoted themselves is yet accomplished may be a matter of opinion, but it has been the repeated taunt of the religious world that Unitarianism is but a system of cold negations, and, whatever the cause, it is beyond question that in recent times many of the more spiritually minded Unitarians have felt less interest in textual criticism and doctrinal controversy, and have believed that the grosser and more material conceptions of God and of His dealings with man are fast passing away, and may safely be left to die a natural death. These men have felt, and felt deeply, that their Unitarianism was a positive faith, and that they had an affirmative Gospel to preach; that their Christian theism was compatible with, if it did not inspire, a pure piety, a lofty morality, and a devout spirituality which they felt constrained to proclaim. In both directions Channing saw there was work to be done. No theologian has more vigorously applied the pruning knife of criticism to the unfruitful branches of his Master's vineyard. No controversialist has refuted the popular dogmas more clearly or bravely than he; but no advocate has stated his opponent's case more fairly and impartially, whilst subjecting it to a searching analysis and proving its mischievous tendency. He did not fail to perceive that men's minds must be freed from creeds and traditions before the spirit of pure Christianity could flourish in them. His own words are, " Much stubble is yet to be burned; much rubbish to be removed; many gaudy decorations which a false taste has hung around Christianity must be swept away, and the earth-born fogs which have long shrouded it must be scattered, before this divine fabric will rise before us in its native and awful majesty, in its harmonious proportions, in its mild and celestial splendour." But though strongly influenced by such convictions whilst taking a retrospective view, Channing's mental and religious outlook was ever forward and upward, and having rejected the Calvinism in which he was reared, he sought the direction of the loftier and more positive phase of Unitarianism, and conspicuously led the way. His writings may be said to form an epoch in the history of religious thought; the lustre that hangs around his name grows brighter with the passing years, and throws its rays over an increasing area and a wider horizon. He discourses on many subjects, illustrating and adorning each that is touched by his pen, though religion seems his favourite atmosphere. On that subject, whether teaching it in its doctrinal or practical aspects, he writes with a special charm. In language the most lucid, a style that never wearies, and with a plainness of speech which all can comprehend, his subject appears to open out before us like the unrolling of a panorama. In perusing his works no intrusive suspicion that philosophy is usurping the place of religion takes possession of the reader's mind; and no fear that superstition lurks behind any conventional phrase disturbs his confidence. In Channing's well-balanced temperament the influences of culture and the impulses of devotion held a joint and even sway with the loftiest reasoning powers. Though he could never brook the view of a plurality of persons on the throne of God, he held the firmest belief in the perfect and spotless character of Christ. He believed in the Divinity of his mission, and that he spoke with supernatural authority. But always that that authority and power were subordinate and derived—not co-equal and co-eternal. He maintained that Trinitarianism has a fatal tendency to degrade the character of the Supreme Being, whilst it places Christ in a light unfavourable to men's piety. He dwells lovingly on the character of God as the concentration of the moral perfections, and contends, with unwavering fervour, for men's personal accountability as opposed to the idea of a vicarious atonement. If there be one thing more than another in connection with religion which is of transcendent interest to man—which thoughtful minds for ever ponder but can never solve—upon which conviction can be founded on faith and hope only—which reason cannot demonstrate, nor experience attest—it is the subject of immortality. Upon that, men yearn for light that may bring their reasoning powers up to the level of their hopes and aspirations. How few are the mortals who can worthily grasp the theme! But who is there that feels that his intellect is not satisfied, that his hope is not transformed into the evidence of things not seen, that his reason and his faith are not harmonized, after a perusal of Channing's discourse on the "Future Life?" But the influence of Channing's works is not restricted to the Unitarian circle. Customary, as to our sorrow we know it is, for our literature to be tabooed by many of those clergymen who are pledged to a stereotyped system of doctrine, we learn from numerous private sources that Channing is largely read in the more liberal sections of Episcopal and Nonconformist orthodoxy. Even in these days of boasted freedom and intellect—Christians are often warned that the free exercise of the faculties God has given them, and will require an account of—is perilous to their souls! But it is an

> Absurd and vain attempt to bind
> With iron chains the freeborn mind,

and there are men both of the clergy and laity who will not endure such fetters—men whose minds may contain their creeds, but whose creeds cannot contain their minds—upon whose shelves and library tables the works of Channing find an honoured place; men to whose souls he, being dead, yet speaketh; and whose lives breathe forth the spirit they have imbibed from a living communion with him. We are here to-night to do honour to the memory of this great man who, born a hundred years ago, may truly be termed an apostle of revived Christianity; one who has done much and will do more to purify the life of the Anglo-Saxon race—to relax the bonds of a corrupted theology, show to men what spirit they are of, and teach those of weaker spiritual insight than himself to see more clearly into the face of their Creator.

ELOGE OF CHANNING.

The Rev. CHARLES WICKSTEED said: A hundred years ago this day week, a New England household received from all-bounteous Heaven, the gift of an infant-life—the growing light of whose purity, nobility, and goodness—after irradiating home, school, college, church, country, and touching at length the four corners of the earth—we are met this day to declare with gratitude, shines still. Sprung from John Channing, a Dorsetshire man of Old England,* the first of the name that came to America, the subject of our éloge to-day had the inherited advantage of some of the best culture and

* Many going from this part of the southern coast of England to America for trade and fishing, the Dorchester Company was formed in 1622, and though it failed, it had more permanent and fortunate successors. No doubt it was on this tide of commercial intercourse that John Channing placed himself in 1712.

opportunity of his country, and as we go back through the intermediate generations, between himself and his English ancestors, we find among them, and among the American families with whom marriage allied them, the merchant, the physician, the lawyer, the member of Congress, the chief justice and the office-bearer of State, and his grandfather, on the mother's side, William Ellery, was one of the Signers of the Declaration of Independence.

His father, who had graduated at the Prince Town College, in New Jersey, became eminent as a pleader at the bar, and was made Attorney-General of his native state. Of a winning countenance and deportment, the law of kindness was in his heart, and on his tongue. He was an obedient son, and a conscientiously good, if somewhat distant, father. Keenly feeling the distresses of mankind, and a generous reliever of them, his munificence was ever accompanied by a sweetness in the manner which doubled the obligation of gratitude. While a warm asserter of the rights of man, he was a lover of peace and order, and though in religious profession particularly attached to the Congregational denomination, and to the ministry of his devout and learned pastor, Dr. Styles, he treated all good men of all denominations with kindness and respect. He generously contributed to the support of Christian worship in the society to which he belonged, and countenanced and encouraged it, not only by a constant and reverential attendance, but by his personal exertions for its institutions, and by his kindness and hospitality.

This admirable father Channing lost when he was 13 years of age.

His mother, Lucy Ellery, was spared to him for more than 50 years after his birth. A disciplinarian in her family, and a woman of energy and judgment, she yet united with these qualities a tenderness of sensibility and an enthusiasm, which threw a charm of romance over her conversation and her actions. Feelings, quick—humour, lively—she so clothed sagacious thought in quaint dialect, that she was as entertaining a companion as she was a wise counsellor. To her son (he himself said) the most remarkable trait in her character was the rectitude and simplicity of her mind. Perhaps, he says, I have never known her equal in this respect. She had the firmness to see the truth, to speak it, to act upon it, and in my long intercourse with her I cannot recall one word or action betraying the slightest insincerity. She had keen insight, she was not to be imposed upon by others; and what is rarer, she practised no imposition on her own mind. There was a rough nobleness in all her ways, which irresistibly won affection and respect, and made her influence good and powerful on all within her sphere.*

In attempting to describe and to trace the mental and spiritual career of Dr. Channing, it would be at once irreverent and ungrateful to the past, and incomplete as regards what followed, not most distinctly to mark these powerful factors in the product. For in this, as in all cases, inherited quality, with the formative

* *See* Memoir of William Ellery Channing, Vol. I.

surroundings which it involves, is the one thing, more than any other, which makes the man. This moment there is no more solemn fact weighing on the conscience of mankind than this law of heredity—and of the two laws of succession, the one to property and the other to quality—the law of succession to special characteristics of body, mind, conscience, and character, is even the more uniform and certainly the more momentous in its operation, of the two.

This, indeed, is not the place or the occasion to enlarge on the wide influence which this fact has on all human life—on the responsibility in which it involves every parent in the Universe—or the weight it brings to bear on the conscience, and the motive-power it supplies to self-culture and the formation of character and habits throughout society. Suffice it that Channing himself believed in the power of this heredity in his own case—that he traced to the virtues of his parents, his own—to their high principles, *his* principles, and that he believed, as he said, that the best part of himself came from them, and from the moral atmosphere they caused him to breathe from the first.

Inherited elements, however, never re-appear in the same combination and proportion in successive generations, but always so vary as to form a new individuality, quite distinct from every other individuality that ever existed, or ever will exist, and that individuality always adds to the result something of its own, something apparently original to itself; and while we trace the high and direct aim, the conscientiousness, the brain power, and the severe purity in the character of Channing to this heredity, the sensitiveness, the aspiration, the severity of self-discipline, and the spirituality that belonged to him, we must trace directly to himself, as the product of his own will, working on the inherited qualities and moulding them into fresh and higher forms—and also must we not, and ought we not to add—to some direct inspiration of heaven, some personal descent and gift of the Holy Spirit on his soul, descending upon him in response to the constant cry of his own heart, and his own daily effort to climb the Mount of God. The result of all these influences, and all this earnest seeking was a rare and unique personality, some leading features of which we shall endeavour to pourtray as we proceed.

But we must not suppose that the external circumstances which helped to make him were exhausted by, though they might be involved in, the immediate heredity of constitution and of home. External Nature herself had a hand in him. The very situation of the place of his birth, Newport, Rhode Island, he himself declares "had no small influence in determining his modes of thought and habits of life." More even than the fresh green pastures on the north side of Newport, with the ever-varying cloud scenery, and softness of the atmosphere, and the reflected light of surrounding bay and ocean, was to him the pebbly, shelly shore on the south, with its gorgeous bi-valves, its shelving sands, its precipitous rocks, the almost perennial roar of the waves, and the deep-riven rent, which formed part of that stern and rock-bound coast,

> "Where the band of pilgrims moored their bark,
> On the wild New England shore."

"No spot on earth," says Channing, "has helped to form me so much as that beach. There I lifted up my voice in praise amidst the tempest. There, softened by beauty, I poured out my thanksgivings and confessions. There, in reverential sympathy with the mighty power around me, I became conscious of power within. There, struggling thoughts and emotions broke forth as if moved to utterance by nature's eloquence of winds and waves. There, began a happiness surpassing all worldly pleasure, as all gifts of fortune—the happiness of communing with the works of God."*

One characteristic incident of his boyhood, and one alone need we pause to describe, and though it has been often referred to and is perhaps better known than anything else recorded of his childhood and youth, it would be a culpable incompleteness in us now to omit it. His father took him to hear a celebrated preacher, from whom the boy

> "With his wonder so intense,
> And his small experience,"

"thought that he should learn great tidings from the unseen world." He heard, however, the usual Calvinism of the time, the decrees, the curse, the darkness, and the

* Sermon on Christian Worship, at Newport. Works. Vol. IV., 339–40 (Ed. 1840).

horror. The boy felt that all amusement and earthly business must now be abandoned, and all people must set themselves to flee, and to help others to flee, from the wrath to come. "Sound doctrine, Sir," said his father to some person after the service. "It is all true, then," said the boy to himself. His father whistled as they drove along, and when he reached home took off his boots, put his feet upon the mantel-piece, and quietly read his newspaper. "It is all untrue," now said the boy to himself. He had been, he thought, the victim of a lie, and from that moment he rose in freedom into the air of heaven to seek God for himself.

And now nothing will arrest the rapidity of our progress through his boyhood and early youth. He read in the public library, and went to the town school which New England Puritanism provided everywhere, that, as it said, "barbarism" might not prevail in their families, and at last to Harvard College,* aided by the same power, that, as it said, "learning might not be buried in the graves of our ancestors."

Here at College the thoughtful, pensive boy pursued

---

* This College had been founded by John Harvard, who, arriving in New England in the year 1638, soon fell a victim to the most wasting disease of the climate, but, desiring to connect himself imperishably with the happiness of his adopted country, bequeathed to the College the whole of his library and one half of his fortune. The State (as well as private persons) also gave liberal aid, as it did to every other great means of promoting education. Indeed, it had been long both the law and the custom of the Puritan settlers, that none of the brethren should allow so much barbarism in their families, as not to teach their children and their apprentices at least to read correctly. Bancroft, I., 459.

his silent and almost solitary walk among the grave moralities, and still graver theologies, of his time, and scarce a trace remains of the more cheerful and refreshing culture of the humaner letters. Living influences and powers seem to have laid no hold of him, or special academic studies drawn his heart. As has been well said, "the intensity of the moral sentiment within him absorbed everything into itself, made his reflective activity wholly predominate over the apprehensive, and determined it in one invariable direction. He meditated where others would have learned, and the materials of his knowledge disappeared as fast as they were given, in the large generalizations of his faith. His mind thus grew while his attainments made no show, and while he missed the praise of learning, he won an affluence of wisdom."* College friendships, few but choice and lasting, college discussions, readings, and debates, a knowledge of the leading standard English divines, and of a few moral philosophers, especially Price and Ferguson, he took away with him indeed, but the fabric of his mind was self-reared, steady alike amidst the black thunder of Calvinism and the encroaching waves of utter overthrow and unbelief. It was quite true what he himself said, "it is easy to read, hard to think," and he chiefly applied himself to the harder task.

From college he went to Richmond, in Virginia, and here we encounter the greatest probably of the formative influences of his youth and early manhood. He was tutor to a dozen boys, and stayed there a

* Prospective Review, Vol. IV. 398.

year and a half. Not insensible to the grace and charms of Southern life and society, when he looked down into the crater on which it rested his soul was filled with horror, and the foundation of his hatred to *slavery* was laid. Retiring also into himself from society, the tone of which offended his Northern Puritanism and principle, he spent much of his time in solitary musing. "I lived alone," he says, "too poor to buy books, spending my days and nights in an out-building, with no one beneath my roof except during the hours of school-keeping. There I toiled as I have never done since, for gradually my constitution sunk under the unremitting exertion." Partly from a youthful stoical enthusiasm, not uncommon, leading him into the practice of asceticism from principle, and partly in order not to use the money, with which his mother had supplied him, but which he thought she herself might want, he deprived himself of necessary food and rest and raiment, became in consequence shyer and shyer of all human intercourse—musing, meditating, introspecting, and self-reproaching—going, in fact, through all the experience so well known in the history of our race, as the discipline of the saint, till his body became a skeleton, and his mind a laboratory of morbid thought, but also of something better than morbid thought. He thus sowed indeed, the seeds of the weakness and disease which never left him, and many have thought that this painful discipline was an utter mistake and wrong, not only to himself, but to society, disabling him from nobler toils and a greater service the remainder of his life. But I am not so sure of this. It was, after all, part of the making of an exceptional man. Health of body, easy circumstances, and peace of mind are not usually the parents of exceptional excellence. Had Johnson been a comfortable gentleman-commoner at Oxford, with good health and competence, enabling him to engage in the society and amusements of the place, instead of a servitor in poverty and neglect, and with a bad constitution, that drove him into solitary ways and studies, are we sure we should have had the great lexicographer and moralist? Who would assert that if Prescot had not lost his sight, he would have produced a better history? Still less who will say, except out of poverty and obscurity and blindness that Milton would have risen into himself? especially after his pathetic lament of "knowledge at one entrance quite shut out," and the inspired prayer, "So much the rather, Thou, celestial light, shine inward."

Even in common life, how often do we find that broken health, adverse circumstances, and disappointment of vainly cherished hopes have driven a man, in spite of himself, into his higher usefulness, and therefore his higher happiness. And so in the self-abnegation and self-mortification of the saint, in the subordination of the physical energies and the passions to the struggle for a purity more than human, and approaching the Divine, who shall say that the special loftiness, and the highest spirituality of a man do not take their rise? The psychology of saintship is as yet an unsettled, nay an almost unexplored, unstudied branch of knowledge. All as far as I know that we have arrived at is this, that the most spiritual states and the loftiest visions that humanity has yet reached, have been in actual connection more or less with these very conditions of what we call morbid asceticism and sense-mortification. And the fact in our own day, that practical and sensible people, and people of the world, find in such a book as the Christian Year a response to the cry of some higher inner nature, and a nutriment for it, indicates the deep natural correspondences there are between the spiritual perfection born of the abnegation of the saint, and the common run of our humanity.

The scanty food, the sleeping on the floor, the shivering in thin thread-bare clothes in the winter frost were no artificial regimen to Channing. These things were the product of a deep yearning. They were the honest outcome of his own nature. His own nature led him to them; his own sense of duty urged him to them. They were the instruments, as he conceived, of his near entrance into the Divine presence, and the realization of his highest visions. He might lose his health by them, but he thought they helped to reveal his own soul to him. Indeed there can be no further question, still less denial, of this after his own words. "Yet I look back on those days and nights of loneliness and frequent gloom with thankfulness. If I ever struggled with my whole soul for purity, truth, and goodness, it was there. There amidst sore trials the great question, I trust, was settled within me whether I would obey the higher or lower principles of my nature; whether I would be the victim of passion, the world, or the free child and servant of God." "My mind was then receiving its impulse towards the perfect."

It is not for us then to step in and say in such a case the self-discipline and self-denial were extreme, unnecessary, undesirable, but to stand in reverence by the holy ground on which that great spiritual conflict was fought; or to ask whether under more judicious self-management we might not have had something better or stronger. One thing is certain, he would not then have been what he was; he would not have been himself, and it is for himself and what he was, not what he might have been, but was not, that we honour and thank him, and canonize him this day. We can easily imagine that as St. Paul, after the great revulsion of his nature, needed his two years' quiet in Arabia, so that Channing after his fierce spiritual conflict, should need a season of repose to restore his health, mature his thought, and gather up the splintered forces of nature before fastening himself to the work of his life. Accordingly from his 20th to his 23rd year he lived in his home of Newport, and at Harvard, where as regent (a kind of head monitor to preserve order), he had a quiet opportunity of following his studies, till at twenty-three he became minister of the Church in Federal Street, Boston, which he rendered so celebrated, and with which he was connected some forty years.

It is not within my design to follow minutely a career which was singularly uniform and uneventful, except in thought and utterance. I prefer rather to study the characteristics of our hero and to try to ascertain how this stately tree grew up.

The political state of society into which he was born had I think an immense influence in the formation of the man. When he was born in 1780, the Declaration of Independence (July 4th, 1776), had only been made four years, and the war between England and America was still going on. (Peace 1782.) Lord Cornwallis was carrying on his hangings of American citizens and the rest of his ruthless proceedings. The recent oppression and tyranny of England was fresh in the minds and frequent on the tongues of all about him, and her harassing and spiteful endeavours to crush the nascent independence of his countrymen, and to force them once again to bow their necks to the hateful yoke they had thrown off were even then filling with sounds of a fiery indignation, the atmosphere into which this child was born. I date to these early influences and surroundings that hatred of injustice and oppression which signalized his afterlife, and caused that humane and gentle nature to flush up with indignation in the presence of any wrong. Thus he was a Republican, not necessarily because that was the best form of government under all circumstances that could possibly be, but because the Republic was to him the mother, and the nurse of Liberty, of Justice, of Happiness, and as he saw her laws developing themselves in the free air into better and better and wiser and wiser completeness, as he saw a native science, a native literature, and a native jurisprudence growing up not only to enrich his country but to win the admiration of the world; as he saw the measureless lands stretch themselves out to afford independence and competence to countless myriads; as he saw the crowds of human beings coming from the hopelessness, and the misery of the old countries with their over-crowded populations, to start a life of hope and energy for generations, in what he now called his own—he was proud of his country, as he had reason to be.

As the early memories, however, of the bitter time of wrong and struggle with wrong, faded before the light of his lofty spirit, and he could remember and appreciate the hearty sympathy of many a manly English statesman and the best half of the English nation during the very time of the war, with the struggle of his country, he could afford to forget and forgive the arbitrary insistance of that brief time on the part of a man and a generation that were past—he took it as an unhappy episode—and going back to the past he cherished a glad pride and affection for that far off little island that had been the home of his fathers, and was by her literature and learning the nurse of his own soul. In truth, Channing saw, and his seeing should carry instruction to all coming time, that the England that then or since, has refused its sympathy to America in any of her great struggles for Justice and Freedom is not the England of the English people. It is in its fulness, or its remains, that Old England that under the Stuarts persecuted and drove away its own children, followed them to their new homes and persecuted them there—annulled their charters, took away their rights, and fought them. And the Englishmen that were thus treated in America left behind them brethren in bonds in England; and for generations we too on this side of the Atlantic have been struggling for our rights, and pressed down under the burdens of our wrongs; compelled to eat dear bread, denied a voice in the representation of our country or the government of our native towns; the doors of our universities shut against our children, marriage made impossible to us except by a compulsory religious service opposed to our tastes and convictions; education offered to us in small doles of charity—Where should I end the list? No! our American brothers fought their battle and won it; we have fought our battle and nearly won it too; but the contest on both sides of the Atlantic has been the same. We are and we always have been on the same side. We are united in the same aims and hopes and sympathies. We ought for ever and for ever to form parts of the same band of progress. Channing saw all this clearly; he knew it was not and never could be the England proper that sought to wrong America or refused her sympathy; he knew it was only the old tyrannical element in it that had sought to wrong Englishmen too. "With this England, the true England, *our* England, we are necessarily," he said, "in a perennial alliance"; and when in 1812 the American Government declared war against England, he almost shrieked out against it as impossible. "It would be the direst blow that we could deal to the progress of all we held good and right—it would be a blow to the progress of the world."

It is curious that, though he seems to have read a good deal, the influence of literature was not great upon him. It was only indeed a small and select part of what he read that he gathered as it were into his mind, or assimilated to his moral being. He does not seem to have cared for what has been happily termed "a general fertilization of the mind." What he read must illustrate or strengthen some grand moral aim of his own or aspiration for humanity, or he did not care about it for any other character of influence. Thus it is astonishing to find him saying after going through almost all the great writers of England up to his own date, "English theology seems to me on the whole little worth; there is little in it to repay the attention of an enlightened mind." But what he meant was that he did not get the idea of Christianity reproduced in its integrity, in the class of writings where it was particularly to be expected it should be found. He acknowledges that he had received help from these sources, for he excepts from the above sweeping censure some thirty or forty writers—among them Butler, Cudworth, Hooker, and Leighton—but he did not find even in these men the free untramelled trusting study and declaration of the truth from which he himself longed for help. He says in language, which for power and explicitness has never been surpassed, referring to every creed-bound, manacled form of establishment, "An Established Church is the grave of intellect; to impose a fixed, unchangeable creed is to raise prison walls around the mind, and when the reception of this creed is made the condition of dignities and rich benefices it produces moral as well as intellectual degradation, and palsies the conscience as much as it fetters the thought. Once make antiquity a model for the future ages, and fasten on the mind a system too sacred for examination and beyond which it must not stray, and in extinguishing its hope of progress you take away its life." (*See* note, p. 172).

I think I know of no writer that owed less to other writers than Channing, or whose religion and thought were more self-originated. This gives his earlier utterances their wonderful freshness and startled the world into some degree of attention. He will never go down to posterity as the author of any system or rank among what are called Scientific Theologians, and such among mankind is the love of argument, the longing for logic, the desire to penetrate into the hidden things of God by a clear metaphysic—to have, in short, a well-sustained and well wrought-out system of thought and belief—however hollow, fanciful, and mistaken may be its basis—such as in fact we find in the works of Augustine and the Institutes of Calvin—that Channing as a theologian, or the author and systematizer of a theology, may have no name and no place in the world's history. While as a thinker, a breather of purity and faith, the imparter to the world of a serene atmosphere of holy Christian reality and health, a great reflection of Jesus Christ, and a bearer on of His pure likeness, he will survive, incorporated into the life of the world, and finding his unconscious immortality in the hearts of generations to come, when the great system writers I have named will only live as specimens of a wasted ingenuity and a false and misleading dogma.

Closely connected with this marked fact in the psychology of Channing, is the adverse criticism sometimes passed upon him, that he was incapable of sustained continuity of thought. I consider his whole life was one continuous course of growing and developing thought. Remember that he was a Christian minister, had the pastorate of a congregation, which that very thought made large, that he was bound through a great part of his life to weekly duty, and that duty was to produce powerful effects in short times and at short intervals. No person of culture and of religious tastes, from the English nobleman to the humblest minister came to Boston without going to drink at this fountain of inspiration. The very success of these concentrated efforts, the very intenseness of these emotional discharges, so to speak, the quick and finished gleams and flashes of his soul absorbed, and all but exhausted, the power of expression in his nature. What could you expect besides, except what you got, the occasional lecture and the occasional review? These were not, indeed, Iliads or Novum Organums, but they sped their way over the United States and Europe, striking chords of an ennobling and enlarging sympathy in thousands of hearts, helping to treasure up great stores of moral result, and forming the noblest continuity of a well-sustained and undeviating purpose. A man may live an epic as well as write one, and may be a philosopher without writing on philosophy, and in this case Coleridge's remark had the right ring about it when he said that Channing was a philosopher in a double sense, for he had the love of wisdom and the wisdom of love, and when I hear not of what he was, but of what he was not, I sometimes wish we could apply to the great heroes of thought and service in their strong and beautiful variety, the spirit of the ever memorable lines of Spenser on the trees—

> "The sailing pine, the cedar proud and tall,
> The builder oak, sole king of forests all,
> The yew, obedient to the Bender's will,
> The birch, for shafts, the sallow for the mill,
> The myrrh sweet-bleeding in the bitter wound,
> The war-like beech, the ash for nothing ill,
> The fruitful olive and the plantain round."

So I wish that some of our critics would open their eyes to the largeness of the world and "see men as trees, walking."

In the numerous estimates of the character of Channing and the influence of his writings, there has come to be an almost monotonous uniformity, arising, however, from a profound unanimity. In truth he was a man most easily interpreted, for he so fully interpreted himself. This has given rise to the charge of iteration, and the charge is true. He was a preacher, and if the preacher does not iterate he cannot create, and will not leave behind him any enduring impression. Is a great deep thought—is an all-underlying principle, to be thrown on the scarcely, perhaps, listening ear of the world *once*, and never repeated? "There is a great deal of iteration in his style," and so there is in the sun's. The sun rises every day and thus iterates itself, but no two days in the life of the world have been the same. And Channing finding the great, but perhaps only half-acknowledged, if half-acknowledged—truth lying day after day deep down in his breast, uttered, and uttered, and uttered it again. But that is no reason that if it has long taken possession of our own minds *we* should go back to the former days of its first formation, and its first fine enunciation. The whole of Channing is not for all of us. For some of us, unquestionably, the half is better than the whole. Because it is a part of his very triumph that he has now made so many of these great truths familiar to us, that they form part of the very atmosphere we breathe. But there are millions and millions yet, to whom I regret to say his is an unspoken Gospel, a much needed, though as yet unheard word.

There is no use attempting to make a mystery of Channing. The simplicity of his aims and methods is transparent; the results are equally clear. He says "Christianity is a revelation of the Infinite universal parental love of God towards his human family." "Receive Christianity as given to raise you in the scale of spiritual being." "There is more danger from thinking too meanly of human nature than from thinking too highly of it." "Expect no good from Christ any further than you are exalted by his character and teachings." "Creeds are to the Scriptures what rushlights are to the sun." "Christianity is a rational religion; if it were not so I should be ashamed to profess it." But "Christianity, we must always remember, is a temper and spirit rather than a doctrine."

But what that doctrine was he had no more doubt than what that spirit and temper were. In the broad sense of the word, from his early manhood to his death he was a Unitarian, and could be, from the principles on which he conducted his inquiries, no other. For he dismissed at once, as unauthoritative, all intervening evidence between himself and Christ, and found, he said, no Trinity in Nature, no Trinity in Reason, and no Trinity in Scripture. And the simple truths of this form of religion, which he regarded as those of the Gospel, he maintained in no merely affirmative style, but put them face to face with the opposing errors, that the nature of both might be clearly seen, and thus, notwithstanding his gentleness and his candour, nay, in consequence of his candour he was, in portions of his writings, about the most vividly incisively controversial of all our great writers on divinity. But he said, "I value Unitarianism not because I regard it as in itself a perfect system, but as freed from many great pernicious errors of the older systems, as encouraging freedom of thought, as raising us above the despotisms of the church, and as breathing a mild and tolerant spirit into all the members of the Christian body."

But he would not, he said, live within the narrow walls of any sect, but under the open sky. As himself had said of Milton "great minds everywhere were his kindred." He would "live in the broad light, looking far and wide, seeing with my own eye, hearing with my own ear, and following truth meekly, but resolutely, however arduous and solitary the path in which she leads." So intensely did he verify each one of his own convictions that he could not admit them afterwards into question, and this gave an air of finality to his mind in later years, not finality for others, or finality for truth, or a conscious finality to his own mental state, but a stillness, settledness, repose—the repose of a stately vessel that had braved perilous seas and encountered many a storm, but was now resting in the harbour of a completed voyage. But they will greatly mistake his spirit who think this meant ultimate completeness, or turn him into a creed-maker for mankind, though I myself should think him, if it were so, the very noblest that has trod this earth since Jesus Christ. But there was nothing of which he himself had a greater dread than stationariness. He declares that he would not linger round his own writings for fear that his mind might become stationary. He rebuked those who spoke of the state of the blessed, of heaven, as stationary; he latterly objected to Unitarianism even that it had become stationary, and now (he writes with displeasure) we have "a Unitarian orthodoxy." He says the Christianity of the primitive age is not the standard for all that follows. "It is growing light and must be expounded by every age for itself." He says, "I am surer that my rational nature is from God than that any book is the expression of His will." It is of the very highest importance that in honouring the memory of this great man, and calling attention to, and circulating in larger and larger quantities his writings, we should bear continually in mind these noble declarations. Already some, a great deal of that new light which he knew must come, has dawned upon us. Already, of many things he has written has that magnificent hope been fulfilled, "I shall see with no emotion, but joy, these fugitive productions forgotten and lost in superior brightness." But although this may be so, he has helped to bring us, and will still help to bring many many more, to the point at which we are ready to receive and waiting for that light. He himself would now spurn us as unworthy spiritual descendants if we were content to remain exactly where he had left us with no new irradiation, no fresh enthusiasm, no opening vision. What! he would say, with all this light of knowledge that has flooded in on your world since I was among you, have you no fresh start to make in the great race? Can you do nothing but slavishly repeat me, using words and arguments that I myself begin to feel are inadequate, if not untrue? I gave you the richest, finest version of the Gospel of Jesus Christ that has reached your ears for eighteen centuries. Are you doing anything to spread it? I put you on the path of a holy and happy progress. Are you moving on it? I left you gifts many of yourselves considered great, and led some sad captivities captive. Are you inspired by my example—are you, with your increased lights and powers, doing for humanity and truth in your day what I strove with all my heart and nature to do in mine?

It is true that in the later years of his life, especially in seasons of depression and sickness, some of the new forms of Scriptural criticism and inquiry struck pain into the nerve of his mental eye, but he braved the pain and would not close the eye. He had confidence in truth, though with his habit of looking at everything as it affected the holiness and happiness of man, he could not himself see how these things were to benefit the race.

But while changes have come over the thought of our time, and on all sides men are rising up to carry on the thought of his, yet his work is far from done, and his good influence far from exhausted on the wisest and the best of us ; while for the masses of Christendom and of humanity it may be made still a star of guidance to prostrate, ignorant millions. What man is there living on the face of the earth who would not rise higher and nobler from the study of that unrivalled decalogue of freedom, each clause of which begins, " I call that mind free "? Are we still beyond or above the word of his power on the misery and wickedness of war? or on the madness and ignobleness of a simply Napoleonic ambition?* Are there no other annexations to be deprecated

* In his Fast and Thanksgiving Sermons he went into the consideration of National dangers and duties bringing Men and Measures to the test of the Christian standard. As a consequence, large numbers of the Laity became indignant with him for what they called his presumption, and his officious intermeddling in matters beyond his sphere. This is always the case, even when

M

besides those of Texas? Does not the very course of our searching physical inquiries still leave room for his voice on the nobleness of man? Has the timid outward and ungenuine conformity of our times no need of the rebuke of his courage and his robust virility? Has God so many faithful children, has Christ so many loving followers, has man so many helpful brothers, have purity and peace so many earnest advocates that we have no further need of him? Listen to what men say of him. The French say he is a new Fénelon; the Germans say he is a new Schleiermacher; Bunsen says that "his work cannot be too highly estimated, and is destined to be a still increasing influence on the spiritual conception of Christianity, and the practical application of its principles." "He is a man like a Hellene, a citizen like a Roman, and Christian like an apostle. If one—whose whole life and conversation in the sight of all his fellow-citizens stand in absolute correspondence with the earnestness of his Christian language and are without a spot—be not a prophet of God's presence in humanity,

the indispensable accompaniment of judiciousness is present, and the very course that helps to build up the minister's character risks it. But double his years and his fame, and he can then say anything he likes. Those who do not approve murmur, if they do murmur, almost inaudibly. The man has become too strong, too trusted, too respected to be put down. So it was in earlier and in later years with Channing. "He witnessed to great truths on the scenes of their violation, and in the presence of the wrong-doer;"* and some of his congregation would not speak to him when they met him in the streets.

---

* Article on Channing's Death. *Christian Teacher*, N.S., vol. V. 105, 1843.

I know of none such." "When first I came across Dr. Channing's writings," says the hardy agriculturist of Scotland, the late George Hope, bred a Calvinist, "I was electrified by them, and felt that he gave a clear, articulated expression to the dim thoughts that had previously floated through my mind, and lifted me nearer to the Infinite Father." Says an early and diligent student of him, in an article in the *Christian Teacher*, published at his death, which is so consummate in its discerning power and truth, that we could not do a greater honour to Channing's memory than republish it, "Perhaps no one living man ever stood in the same spiritual relation to so many minds." "The doctrines of Jesus were the lights in which he regarded the relations of every human being to society and to God, and consequently his judgments on moral subjects were uttered with a simplicity, a commanding clearness and fulness of conviction that make them sound like inspirations." "He spoke like a prophet as from immediate vision, as one who had come from listening to the everlasting voice." So nearly unparalleled was his influence even on minds of a very high order, that the Italian professor Sbarbaro says that "no single writer since Dante has ever made so great an impression on my faculties as Channing," and he speaks of the rapid and universal diffusion of his works in all corners of the civilized earth.

Very numerous are the tributes to his greatness and his influence which I have collected at some pains, but which a regard to your time and patience compels me to omit.

together, I may say, with a great deal of other matter which I had prepared. These testimonies come from the leaders of thought, and they come from almost every land—from America, from England, from France, from Holland, from Italy, from Switzerland, from Germany, from Transylvania, and each year they increase in volume and significance, from the first response of sympathy sent by the Unitarians in this country, more than half a century ago to the other day in London, when Monsieur Rénan wrote of him "that he had heard the first sounds of the bell of the future Gospel," and as one of the grandest of those saints whom Rome had not yet canonized. Almost as numerous, too, are the editions that have been published of the whole or portions of his works, and of the translations that have been made of them into foreign tongues, and at this moment, as a further instalment, the spirited step has been taken to offer to the world a new edition of 100,000 copies.

Ought we to let the centenary year of his birth pass by without gratitude to God, without gratitude to this his servant, and a renewed desire, with renewed encouragement, to spread far and wide those pure influences by which the souls of so many of us have been raised and blessed, and with which we must try to baptize the nations?

Rev. WILLIAM GASKELL said : Ladies and gentlemen, they will be very few words with which I shall trouble you. I am sure you will all feel with me that we are deeply indebted to our "old friend Mr. Wicksteed" for having come so great a distance to help us on this occasion, and for the interesting, spirited, and excellent address which we have listened to with so much pleasure, and I would hope with profit too. In that address he brought out with great clearness and force the leading characteristics of Dr. Channing's life and work, those which made him most deserving of honour, and in a way so well fitted to excite our sympathy and make us enter into his spirit. He referred to various tributes to Dr. Channing which had been paid by eminent men. There is one which always strikes me as most appropriate, that of the poet Whittier, who said "He was one of Heaven's anointed men." When the Chairman referred to his writings finding their way to the shelves and tables of many of our orthodox friends, it recalled to my recollection what once occurred to a good lady, a member of the Cross Street congregation, who went to visit some orthodox friends in the north of Lancashire. She found that they were full of admiration for a young minister who had just come to settle amongst them, and who had charmed them by his eloquent discourses. On the Sunday morning they asked her if she would like to go with them to their place of worship. She said that she should; and on their return home they wished to know how she had liked the young minister's sermon. To which she replied, "I liked it so much that I have read it more than once." Seeing that they looked rather incredulous, she said, "If you doubt my word I will send you the volume which contains it, and you can read it for yourselves." This she did, when, to their surprise, they found that the sermons which had charmed them so much were, with very slight alteration, Dr. Channing's. It is certain that his writings have done far more than those of any other writer amongst us to clear away that charge, to which the chairman referred, so often formerly brought against our pure and simple faith, that it was a cold and heartless system of belief. But I must not enter on this subject. I have been requested to ask that this great meeting should bear some fruit. As you are aware, we have been gathered together at the instigation of the Manchester District Unitarian Association. That Association seeks to do its work in the large, free, and generous spirit which characterised Dr. Channing. As its president for a number of years, I can, without hesitation, say that its great object has been, not to build up a sect on any narrow, selfish ground, but to make more widely known what we hold to be the truth as it is in Jesus, unadulterated by the foreign elements with which in the course of ages it has got mixed up, and to extend the bounds of that Holy Catholic Church, in which the spirits of the pure and true and free, however differing in opinion, may all worship together. But I shall be breaking my promise if I go on talking to you. I will content myself, therefore, with simply asking those of you in the District who are not already subscribers to the Association to become so at once; and thus show your sympathy with the great, good man, the centenary of whose birth we are met to celebrate. I have great pleasure in moving that our best thanks be given to Mr. Wicksteed for his kindness in having come amongst us, and for the excellent address which he has delivered to us.

Mr. DENDY said: Mr. Chairman, ladies, and gentlemen, by some mistake, I apprehend of the printers, Mr. Gaskell and myself were put down to make a speech each. This was not what we were asked to do, and I can assure you it is not what I intend to do. I simply wish to second the vote of thanks to Mr. Wicksteed for his very able, faithful, and discriminative Eloge on Channing. It is our honour to belong, nominally at least, to the same section of the Christian Church to which Channing belonged. He and we alike call ourselves Unitarians, but I have altogether mistaken the character of Channing if his dogmatic Unitarianism was that which lay deepest in his heart. Mr. Wicksteed has rightly brought out that he was in spirit much more a Christian than anything else. In his spirit we also can follow Christ, though in details we may differ somewhat from his theology. For his theology, though perhaps more conservative than ours, was progressive in its nature, and that is the nature of our theology of the present day. I will not attempt any praise of Channing. For me to do so after what has been said would be absurd. I will only quote the words of a great American poet, and try to apply it to our own position. Longfellow writes, and this, I think, is the moral to be drawn from all great lives

> "Lives of great men all remind us
> We may make our lives sublime,
> And departing, leave behind us,
> Footprints on the sands of time."

Now, it is not for us, possibly not for one in this large assembly, to leave any footprints such as those which Channing left, but it is for us to help on the cause which he loved, and much as I think it would have gratified him to know that 100 years after his birth his spirit should be honoured by such a meeting as this, and by many other such meetings, I believe his heart would have felt more closely drawn towards the work which we have in hand; when I say that I refer to the Association which has called us together to-night. If he could see some of those small hard-working, striving congregations in what are called our back slums; if he could see the good work there being done; if he could see how the spirit of true Christianity, of true charity, towards all men of all sects is being taught, he would feel a livelier emotion of gratification than could be aroused by the largest meeting in the most beautiful hall and with the most excellent music. I ask you then, and I urge you strongly to do what you can to strengthen these associations. If they were dogmatic associations; if the Unitarian Associations were mere dogmatic affairs attacking the Trinity, I for one should not care to be connected with them—but this is not their work. As Mr. Gaskell has said, their work is to infuse the spirit of Christian life, and Christian life independent of sects, and if not altogether independent of theology, at least never allowing their theology to override their Christian life and charity. I hold in my hand an appeal from the Manchester District Unitarian Association for Missionary Purposes, and I hnmbly and earnestly ask all of you to do something for this Association. If you would only sometimes visit those little places of worship, if you could see the faces of toil-worn but earnest-minded men who there assemble to do their best to encourage each other to lead a Christian life, I am sure your hearts would warm towards them and you would not feel comfortable or happy in your own beautiful places of worship unless you had contributed somewhat to sweeten the life and lighten the toil of those missionaries of free thought—those missionaries of the pure gospel of Christ. I now beg to second the proposition that our most hearty and cordial thanks be given to Mr. Wicksteed for his most excellent discourse.

Professor ROSCOE said: Mr. Chairman, ladies and gentlemen, the task I have to perform is a very pleasant and simple one, and one which I am sure will meet with your approbation. It is to propose a vote of thanks to our worthy chairman, Mr. Alderman Grundy, for the able way in which he has conducted the business of this meeting, and especially for the very able and appropriate introductory address, with which he was kind enough to favour us. Perhaps I may be allowed to make one remark with regard to the occasion on which we are now assembled. Channing, as it appears to me, was a very many-sided man. We have heard a very full and clear account of Changing's work in one direction. I should wish to point out that as a leader in education, I believe he was no less great than as a theologian and expositor of Christian life. It was owing greatly to him, and to the energy with which he pursued the matter, that America took the position, which I think we may say she still occupies, in the forefront of educational progress. I am sure you will all remember the words with which Channing speaks about the education of the poor. It was only the other day that here in Old England we came to the conclusion, as a nation, that it was necessary the poor should be educated. The step we have just taken America took years ago, and what America did I believe was greatly due to the energy and influence of Channing. "The poor man," says he, "as to his natural capacity, does not differ from others. He is equally susceptible to improvement. Our institutions demand this general diffusion. Liberty requires that every citizen should have the means of elevation. Men in other countries have been fighting to be sovereigns. Here every man *is* one. Every citizen participates in legislating for the commonwealth and in administering the government. Ought not every man, such duties devolving on him, to receive as liberal a training as possible?" Not only, however, was Channing active in the cause of promoting what we now call primary education. He laboured also to raise the character of the higher education in America. He was long connected with Harvard, and remained for a number of years on its governing body, and in this direction also we may see the influence which Channing exerted, for surely there is no other country in the world where riches, if made so quickly have been so well spent, as in America, for there is no country in which it has become so completely the custom for the rich men to spend their money in benefiting succeeding generations by the foundation of great institutions. We are now beginning to learn something of this in England. We have our Owens, our Beyers, our Masons, and Firths. But for one such name which we can mention in England, our American friends tell us they can count a dozen. This general appreciation of the value of the higher education in the United States is greatly due to the influence which Channing exerted, and for these reasons it gives me pleasure to bear witness to the satisfaction with which all interested in the progress of education in this country welcome these celebrations of the Channing Centenary.

Mr. E. C. HARDING said: I beg to second the vote of thanks to Mr. Alderman Grundy for presiding on the present occasion. The speeches we have listened to this evening take some of us back many years, when Channing's noble and inspiring addresses were fresh in our minds, and when our hopes were raised high that they might produce great results in the world; and to me our proceedings this evening are like visiting some cherished spot of one's childhood with which sacred memories are associated. Some of the aspirations which are embodied in Channing's addresses have been realized —slavery in the United States is now a thing of the past. The appeals he made against unnecessary war have been less heeded, but there are indications that those too will be accomplished. Who can doubt that the fourteen eventful days through which we have just passed have made it impossible for any government to commit this country to an unjust or unnecessary war? If we are faithful to our trust we too may expect to see a more general acceptance of the simple truths of the gospel for which he pleaded so eloquently and earnestly.

[Note to Mr. Wicksteed's Eloge, referred to on p. 154. . . . If the influence of English Literature, as he has described it, was confessedly not great upon him (though of course he did not include in his slighting remarks such writers as Bacon, or such poets as Shakespeare or Milton) the influence of the special literature of his own country on his mind must be put down as almost *Nil*. Indeed such a literature could scarcely be said to exist. Great and full of power and genius as it has become since, it could be hardly said to be born when Channing was born, and he himself on the contrary is to be regarded as one of its creators and inspirers instead of one of its children. It is right indeed, to gather up (as Duyckinok has done in his Cyclopædia of American Literature), and with reverent hand, all the early efforts of a Nation to express its own thought and feeling, to sow the seeds of a Literature of its own—and to preserve with tender respectfulness every scrap in prose and verse of a hundred writers—yet all this does not seem to have had a traceable influence on the mind of Channing or his style. Jonathan Edwards, no doubt permeated the atmosphere in which he was born; but he had only to grow up to early youth to throw him off for the Philosphers of Free Will and Moral Sentiment. The clear common sense, and manly style of Benjamin Franklin, Jefferson, and Adams, cannot have been without some effect, and Lindley Murray was unquestionably a power in America as well as in England. Though Bishop Berkeley and the much misrepresented and misjudged Thomas Paine, are sometimes claimed as American writers—the accident of having lived part of their lives and published part of their works in America, scarcely entitles them to this distinction. The only two men and writers on his native soil that I can recognize as having direct spiritual analogies with Channing—and that chiefly on the philanthropic and humanitarian side of his character—were Lindley Murray and Dr. Benjamin Rush. Dr. Rush, born 1745, besides four volumes of Medical Inquiries and Observations, and many other medical publications, wrote Essays on Literary, Moral, and Philosophical topics, on the Amusements and Punishments proper to Schools, opposed corporal punishment and hanging, was one of the earliest friends of the Temperance cause, tried to improve prisons, gave his Sunday Fees entirely to charity, and wrote "The Paradise of the Negro Slave: A dream. An Appeal for Humanity to the African," and yet I do not remember a single allusion by Channing to his existence. Lindley Murray, born 1745, besides his well-known Grammar and English Speaker, published an essay on the "Power of Religion on the Mind, in Affliction, and on the Approach of Death," for whose continued and gratuitous circulation after his decease he provided, leaving his property for liberating and providing for (freed) slaves, and promoting the civilization of North American Indians.

But Channing's style, as well as his thought and character, was entirely his own. It was perfectly perspicuous and perfectly polished. It was classical in the best sense of the word, uniting force with refinement—absolutely free from "Tall Talk," and every provincialism and vulgarism. As we once heard the late Lord Carlisle say, "He found good manners the same everywhere, whether in London, Paris, Boston, or St. Petersburg," so Channing's language was that of cultivated Englishmen everywhere—unspoiled even by the temptation of the pulpit to exaggeration. Turn from any author to Channing, and you find him easy and natural though studied, unstrained and flowing yet solid—no jerks, no awkwardnesses, no false pauses—no endlessnesses, no bewildering parentheses, no complications—choice, but not unwonted words—no rhetoric as such, but always clear and firm and fervent. Add virility to the saintliness of Fra Angelico's figures, and you have the spiritual form of Channing. He helped unquestionably to give Boston a right to the name of the "Athens" of America, and to inaugurate the splendid host of writers which accompanied and followed him in time. For it must be remembered that Washington Irving, Fenimore Cooper, Charles Sprague, Mrs. Sigourney, Everett, Bryant, Palfrey, Ticknor, Prescott, Sedgwick, Bancroft,

Seward, Emerson, Longfellow, Whittier, Hawthorne, Wendell Holmes, Palfrey, Motley, Lowell, Bayard Taylor, Mrs. Stowe, in general literature, besides other great writers in special departments, and a large and goodly company of divines and preachers and philanthropists and orators were all born after Channing.]

THE LIVERPOOL MEETING.

The centenary of the birth of Dr. Channing was celebrated on Wednesday evening at St. George's Hall by a large and brilliant assemblage. The celebration commenced with an excellent tea, during which a selection of music was performed. Besides this, there was a very interesting exhibition of microscopes and other objects. Mr. H. A. Bright presided in the early part of the meeting, and was succeeded by Mr. W. H. Meade-King. There were also present the Revs. Charles Beard, B.A., G. Beaumont, W. Binns, W. H. Dallinger, G. Fox, H. W. Hawkes, T. Holland, E. Howse, T. Lloyd Jones, J. Lee, D. Davies, E. Hassan, J. E. Odgers, M.A., C. J. Perry, B.A., R. Pilcher, B.A., H. S. Solly, M.A., J. H. Thom, and S. F. Williams; and Messrs. A. Booth, F. H. Boult, C. T. Bowring, C. Botterill, Wm. Bowring, G. F. Chantrell, J. B. Cooke, Chas. Dyall, J. T. Ellerbeck, H. Fernie, H. M. Guthrie, F. H. Gossage, W. Holland, W. D. Holt, Geo. Holt, H. Jevons, Dr. J. M. Johnson, C. W. Jones, E. English, T. Goffey, T. E. Paget, R. Robinson, J. Samuelson, H. Tate, J. C. Thomson, W. Thornely, W. E. Turner, H. Young, &c.

Mr. T. E. PAGET said that Mr. H. A. Bright had, some time ago, kindly promised to occupy the chair, but owing to serious illness at home his presence was very much wanted there. In order, however, not to disappoint them, Mr. Bright had very kindly consented to come down for a short time. He felt sure that he might tender to Mr. Bright, in the name of the meeting, their warm sympathies, together with the earnest hope of each and all that his son would very speedily be restored to health.

Mr. H. A BRIGHT said: It was with reluctance that I accepted the honour of presiding here to-night. I had personal and very sad reasons for wishing to abstain from any festivity at present; and especially was I anxious that Mr. William Rathbone should fill this chair, that we might have the great advantage of his presence, and that we might show him in what respect his old friends and constituents have always held him. Another, indeed, may now occupy that seat in Parliament which was so long his, but no other can take the place he holds in all our hearts, or obliterate the memory of one who, beyond almost any one I have ever known, thirsted for the right and had learned to deaden love of self. And now, ladies and gentlemen, turning to the occasion of our meeting to-night, and the transition scarcely seems to me a violent one, we are met to commemorate the day when, one hundred years ago, William Ellery Channing was born. And this centennial celebration of Dr. Channing is surely a very remarkable occurrence.

That there should be such a celebration in the case of some great poet, whose burning words have sunk deep into the minds of his fellow-countrymen is intelligible enough. That the anniversary of some great victory, when a nation has achieved her freedom, or a tyrant has been crushed, should be held in honour, is a matter of no surprise. But why, in the very midst of present political strife should men in London, Manchester, and Belfast, and a few days later on, we in Liverpool, meet together in honour of an American theologian? Why is the name of Channing being commemorated alike in the city of the Pontiffs, and amid the poor dwellings of the capital of Iceland? Well, I suppose there is but one answer, the only one and the true one. It is because men feel that they owe Channing a distinct debt of gratitude which they would only too thankfully repay, though they well know that recognition, and not repayment, is alone now possible. Nearly ninety years have passed since Dr. Priestley (and I wish to pay a passing homage to one to whom modern Unitarians, certainly not men of science, have been perhaps a shade unthankful) was driven from his home by a Church and State mob, and took refuge in the freer lands across the seas. He was a good and true man, if ever there was one, kindly and genial, a great scholar, a learned theologian, an illustrious philosopher, and, above all, a confessor, almost a martyr, for conscience sake, yet Priestley's name fails to stir us like the name of Channing. Channing was twenty-four years old when Priestley died, but I doubt whether in any case he owed much to his teaching. But other influences had already been at work, and not the least, the influences of the all-pervading Mother Nature. As Channing, still a youth, paced the rocky shores of his native state, Rhode Island, he drank in the spirit of freedom and devotion from the wind and wave. The influence of such a scene had been felt centuries before by the old British monk Morgan, who was known afterwards as Pelagius, because, so tradition tells us, he was constantly seeking fresh inspiration from the *Pelagos* or ocean, and who was in his time the champion of the freedom of the human will, as Channing was in later times. One had St. Augustine for an opponent, the other had the Calvinism of Jonathan Edwards, and both first learned the lesson of freedom from the sights and sounds of the natural world. But that strand on which Channing walked, had a special association of its own. It was a part of that coast, where, in the year 1620,

"A band of pilgrims moored their bark
On the wild New England shore!"

They had fled from ecclesiastical tyranny, and Channing would not that any ecclesiastical tyranny, of any kind or sort, should still remain. "Freedom to worship God" should be absolute and uncontested. And now let me say, in a few words, what I conceive to be Channing's chief claim to our gratitude, our respect, our veneration. It is not that he held certain speculative opinions which we call Unitarian, though, as a matter of fact he has done more to spread those opinions than any one man before or since. But, in the first place, I doubt whether those of us who agree most fully with Channing's speculative opinions, admire him chiefly on that account, and I doubt not there are many here who do not agree with these opinions, and who think they err, either by defect or excess, either going too far, or not going far enough. Nor is it as a great man of letters that we admire him. His writings are all condensed into that wonderful little one shilling edition. He wrote no great book; nothing but a few essays, a few lectures, and a good many sermons. His style is pure and dignified, but somewhat diffuse, and only at times reaches to any great height of eloquence. And yet how noble is his appreciation of Fénélon, how sympathetic his character of Milton, how scathing his denunciation of Napoleon. Still, on the whole, there have been many far greater men of letters, for whom no centennial would ever be suggested. No, the reason of our regard is the greatness of Channing's character. It is not for what he did, or for what he thought, but for what he was that we hold him so high in our affections. I believe him to have been one of the best men who ever lived, and it is his example, rather than his teaching, which is influencing men for good to-day. There is a well-known passage in Goethe's *Wilhelm Meister*, where the education of the young is to be taught symbolically, and the recollection of this comes to me as I think of Channing. The first lesson is to look upwards—it is the lesson of reverence for what is above. Channing learnt this lesson early, and teaches it to us. He had for the moment to help to destroy old forms of faith, but he would "uproot the false by planting of the true." His very process of destruction was a process of construction, and meanwhile, there was no frivolity or flippancy in the means he used or the words he spoke; the truths he held were sacred to him with a sanctity beyond expression. Nothing base or bad could, we are told, live in his presence for a moment. He had looked up, and learned to reverence what was above. And the second lesson, according to *Wilhelm Meister*, was to look down, and reverence what was below. Channing found the curse of slavery heavy on the land, and his first impulse was to leave the question to others to settle. But he looked down, and he saw the dignity of man debased beneath the foot of the slave owner, and he resolved to uplift it not alone for the sake of the individual, but for the sake of human nature. And so with men of despised opinions. No one could have had less sympathy than he with Theodore Parker's special views, but he would have no one insulted on account of his views, and so in defence of Parker he risked the good opinion of his fellow ministers, as in the case of slavery he had risked the good opinion of his fellow citizens, and of the leading laity of his church. And lastly the pupil of the story had a third lesson to learn—of reverence to himself and the facts around him. He must now look straight onward, ready to act on his own convictions, and bear his part as one of many. And Channing was now indeed foremost and most earnest among those of his time—among those of *any* time.

> " Whose one bond is that all have been
> Unspotted by the world."

He had learned the three great lessons of the three forms of reverence—piety, compassion, and earnestness. By these moral gifts his preaching became so powerful for good, that long before he died he had become one of the strongest influences in New England. And when he died his charity was felt to have been so wide, that the Roman Catholics were touched at the thought of it, and tolled the bell of their cathedral when his body was carried to its last home. And then it was that here in England, as I am old enough to remember, a sense of loss came upon us all, and in all our chapels sermons were preached to remind us that our greatest leader had fallen. But to-night, ladies and gentlemen, we will not think of what we lost when Channing died, but of what we gained when he was born. If *Southey*, the High Churchman could speak of him in the *Quarterly Review*, as " an honour to any age and any country," what must be our feelings towards him. It is for us to imitate his example, to spread his teachings, and to show our gratitude not in barren words but fruitful deeds.

THE REV. J. H. THOM'S ADDRESS.

WE hold our celebration to-night under accidents of disadvantage. We are behind time. The Hour and the Man have not come together at the exact moment. Duties to the nation might, it was apprehended, be agitating the atmosphere on the 7th of April, duties which Channing would have regarded as supreme, above all personal considerations, but which might not have contributed to the calm depths of contemplation in which alone his spiritual image may be mirrored and seen. Yet, perhaps, it was unfortunate, for if we could not have been gladdened and purified by strength added here to a cause which he had most at heart, brotherhood with weaker races, and detestation of oppressive wars, we might have been lifted by his spirit far above local or temporary defeat to regions of faith where righteousness and mercy universally prevail. And not only are we late in the field, but mighty reapers have been there before us, gathering the richest sheaves and presenting them in perfect assortment, so that we are only the poor gleaners of what they have left. This, indeed, would be positive gain to us to-night, for the field is of inexhaustible richness and variety, if we could presume that every one here was familiar with all that has been said at London, at Manchester, and elsewhere, and we had but to follow the steps of our leaders to gather up what even their full arms could not hold in one embrace, and add something more of a finishing hand to uncompleted work. That we lose to-night something of the freshness of the occasion, that all the essential things have been already said, and in the best way, does not disconcert us; rather do we gladly appropriate it all to enrich our own offering, for we are here only to bear a continuous testimony, to pay *our* share of the greatest debt that man can owe to man, to swell with grateful voice the almost universal tribute to the friend and benefactor of their souls from English-speaking people, and not English only, but German, French, Italian, Hungarian, and even Spanish speaking people. Whether Spain has other translations I do not know; but I do know that fifty years ago Blanco White had the Harvard "Discourse on the Evidences of Christianity," translated into Spanish.

And speaking of our debt of gratitude, this generation cannot well know how great it was, nor recall that unparalleled testimony to him in the sudden sinking of the heart in every friend of Light and Liberty on both Continents when his death was known, as though every evil cause was stronger, every righteous cause weaker than before. Wellington said that the presence of Napoleon in the field was equal to the difference of thirty thousand men; but here the loss was of *the only man* who in every righteous cause could make his voice heard in both worlds, the Old and the New. The greatest soldier when he is dead gains no more victories; the great Prophet lives for ever in a widening triumph, though the world should not know from what hand, from what voice, the impulse was received,—and of *us* who have been for more than fifty years under the unspent impulse of his quickening light, few now living can remember its first electric stroke. I remember it. I remember a sense as of being new-born. I cannot speak worthily of Channing, but I can acknowledge my debt. Others had taught me much; no one before had unsealed the fountain in myself. He was the first to touch the spring of living water, which made me independent even of himself. That is an obligation never to be forgotten; with which none other can compare. I speak of myself, as among the first on this side of the ocean to receive the impact of his mind, only to illustrate what he was to so many; the opener of a new religious life, not as the founder of a school, but as a destroyer of all schools except the school of the spirit. About 1825, fifty-five years ago, I was living a severe but salutary life in the North of Ireland, little more than a boy, teaching seven hours a day in the great classical school of the Belfast Royal Institution, and for the rest of the working day going through my college course as a student under the professors, whose lecture rooms were in another department of the same building. I was living familiarly with scholars, of a race of scholars, the Bruces and the Hinckses, admirable and venerable men, walking in the light of their own convictions straight as a line, though, perhaps, rather as devout servants under the Old Covenant than as dear children under the New. They were Arians; the only preaching I had heard up to that time was Arian, and Arianism being then upon its trial, about to be disowned and cast out by 'the Presbyterianism of Ulster, was, as a learned school, making its appeal to external and textual foundations, not having, not knowing that it had, the predominant spring of its being in what may be briefly set forth as the one distinctive note, the root-principle of Channing's Christianity—that all souls are of one Family. I remember how that light first came to me, and set me free for ever; nor have I a more vivid recollection than of turning for a moment from weary work to steal a glance at the tract on Milton's Treatise on "Christian Doctrine," which the College-porter had just laid upon my school desk, and of being carried out of myself and my surroundings by its first lofty words:—" Endowed with gifts of the soul which have been imparted to few of our race, and conscious of having consecrated them through life to God and mankind, he rises without effort or affectation to the style of an Apostle: 'JOHN MILTON TO ALL THE CHURCHES OF CHRIST, AND TO ALL WHO PROFESS THE CHRISTIAN FAITH THROUGHOUT THE WORLD, PEACE, AND THE RECOGNITION OF THE TRUTH, AND ETERNAL SALVATION IN GOD THE FATHER, AND IN OUR LORD JESUS CHRIST.'" It was said, by one who had near opportunities of knowing him, that, like Milton, Channing himself lived and died an Arian. I know nothing of that; I care nothing for that,—and if it was so, neither did he, for in all his writings as he left them to the world there is but one teaching, that whatever may be the differences of spiritual rank, there are no root-differences of spiritual natures, that the spirit of the loftiest archangel and of the lowliest child of man are in the same relation to the Father of Spirits, separated by no impassable limits, sons of one family. You here in Liverpool, who for half a century have been under the influence of Mr. Martineau's teaching, never felt as *new* the method of spiritual growth which Channing instituted. But hear Mr. Martineau himself acknowledging his own debt, thirty-seven years ago, when Channing died: "Poor and paltry were it to deny our dependence upon him, and pretend even in relation to our faith that we are above the influence of such authority as his; not to feel it were to be cold to the most earnest wisdom and the most penetrating love. By the Divine right of sanctity and virtue, he was as a master among us. He did not impose upon us *his* faith, but he awakened and revealed our own."* Hear also to the same effect John James Tayler, a kindred spirit, if ever there was one: "The name of Channing will henceforth be indissolubly associated with the history of a new era in religious opinion.—He forsook criticism to enforce and apply to the living wants of the human soul those great eternal truths which criticism had already evolved, purified, and indicated. He seized the grand universal principles of Christianity, as they presented themselves to his meditative intellect on the broad page of the Divine Word,—and stepped forth with the intrepidity of spirit which ever accompanies the consciousness of great principles,—to revise the interests which an age of revolution and scepticism had cast into unmerited ne-

---

* "The Christian Teacher." Vol. for 1843.

glect, to inspire the love of truth and right for their own sakes, to exalt virtue above utility, to restore Religion to its proper seat among the warmest affections of the human heart, to plead for universal justice and freedom, to inculcate a boundless trust in the wisdom and benignity of the Universal Father, to teach us, in the largest and noblest sense, to 'honour all men.'" *

In a word, what did Channing do for us? He lifted Religion out of the region of controversy; out of the region of criticism; out of a wrangle of texts and an arithmetical computation of on which side the balance lay; out of polemics into spiritual discernment; out of the disputable and limited letter to the self-manifesting and inexhaustible light of the glory of God shining in the face of Jesus Christ. He, more than any one man, did for as many of us as were groping amid beggarly elements what the Divine Teacher desired to do for the Jews of his day:—"Ye search the Scriptures, and in *them* ye think ye have eternal life—but they are they that testify of *Me*, and ye will not come to Me, to have the life direct." This is what Channing did for the Church to which he belonged, and for all who would hear his voice. He rose from the dead word to living Persons. He emancipated us from external and traditional methods, from the cerements of the Creeds that embalmed bodies of divinity from which the life was gone, to be taught afresh by the Father of Spirits, and by his living Word. We are reminded, it is true, even

* "The Christian Teacher." Vol. for 1843.

by those who place him first, that he was not a critic, nor a great scholar, a learned theologian versed in the verifying methods of historical investigation, and intimately acquainted with all ancient religions. Be it so: the same, I suppose, might be said without loss of reverence and indebtedness of a Greater than he; but I have seen it laid down by the highest living authorities upon these matters, that "the result of the modern critical testing of the literary and historical value of the New Testament documents is this,—that it has brought back the living Christ to the world; that it has inaugurated a second coming of the Son of Man; that it has caused the spiritual facts of history to take the place of scholastic systems." Now, that is exactly the result which Channing reached *per saltum*, not by a critical but by a spiritual method, by real personal relations with God and Christ. All honour to criticism in its place; but at its best it only clears the way to unobstructed vision, where there is a spiritual eye to see; and for smothered and muffled sounds, confusing reverberations from the ages, broken and faint echoes of an echo, gives us the real evidence, and opens a spiritual ear to the Divine voice anew. Channing searched the Scriptures for himself, and the spiritual discernment that was in him discriminated the imperishable parts as a magnet discriminates steel filings, or rather, for the figure is too outward, what is spirit and life in *them* struck deeper the living roots in himself already planted by God, found them there and fed them,—and all else, however interesting in other human lights, was to the soul of no essential value. We follow Channing, we honour him as a master for all Israel, not on account of his opinions, but on account of his method. Many things helped to quicken him; nothing intercepted, nothing stood between him and the face of God. The humblest of men, he would not make humility a mean excuse for shrinking from the divine calling and arduous birthright of his nature. The light might shame him, or condemn him, but for that very reason would he stand in the light. Conscious of his own imperfections because his standard was so high, holding his attainments in truth and in goodness to be as nothing in comparison with the life indeed, he would not on that account in spurious humility evade the severe responsibilities of a child of God, nor call the ignoble forfeiture of his place, what Dante branded as "the great refusal,"—lowliness and piety.

And, now, having acknowledged my personal debt, I shrink from changing my attitude, to weigh, or estimate, or determine the permanent place in religious history of the Benefactor of my spirit. I shrink from any attempt to take the bearings, and define the action of great minds. To receive their influence, to be strengthened by their power, and even to feel conscious that their highest thoughts have independent roots in ourselves is a profound joy, but to leave this position with the view of compassing and describing such minds would for me, at least, be unbecoming, and instantly to fall from a sublime sense of fellowship into self-humiliation and pain. Thirty-seven years ago I had to speak of Channing from the pulpit and the press, because the offices I then held towards the Pulpit and the Press required me so to do, not as a critic, for the awe of his greatness and his loss was then fresh upon us, but as a witness and a narrator, and I know not that I could succeed better now, for there is this peculiarity in the action of great minds, that no distance of time alters your relation towards them. You may know all their thoughts, and the power of those thoughts have passed into your life,— but not the power of transmitting that power. As often as you approach themselves again the magic of their touch still makes you sensible that their place is not yours, and that the magician's wand cannot be taken out of his own hand. This unchangeable relation is a delight, not a trouble of soul, so long as you are not brought into a false attitude towards a great man; but when made very unhappy at the thought of having to speak of Channing on an occasion like this, feeling that it is an occasion which ought to be conspicuously honoured throughout all England, but thinking that one collective celebration at the North might have sufficed, in my fear and trembling what might afford a happy way out of my trouble occurred to me, and it was this— first, to let Channing himself speak of his works, all that we have of him, according to his own view of their significance and of the necessity that existed for them; and secondly, to let him be seen as he was seen by one of his peers, to set him in the focal light of a spirit that was the equal of his own. And both methods of portraiture were ready at hand. Only the year before his death Channing issued his collected works, with an elaborate preface setting forth what he deemed their essence, and how much of himself he had put into them. And I have, and have given to the world, his Correspondence with one whom alone, as far as I know, he approached with the deference of one who came to learn. With a larger experience than his, with vaster opportunities and acquirements in scholarship, in general knowledge, in criticism, in philosophy and theology, in ecclesiastical history;—in spiritual sensibility, and discernment, Blanco White was not his inferior,—yet Blanco White said of him just what at the time we all were saying, that on all that is vital, and eternal, and actuating in Christianity, on all that touches our relations to humanity, Channing could raise him, in whatever illness and weakness, to his highest exaltation of feeling, and speak to his conscience as with the voice of God. This is a great testimony from an old and suffering man to whom nothing in sacred literature, nothing in the moralists or orators of antiquity, was unknown. In one place he writes to Channing, "With such pain and difficulty I guide my pen that nothing but absolute necessity has forced me to undergo the fatigue of writing"—and this is the necessity—"The last work of yours on Slavery has filled me with such spirits that I must write. It appears to me to rise above argument, and to derive its powers of conviction from an intuition of our own nature beheld in the intimate connection of God with our souls. I hope I am not employing vain words. I should think very lowly of any one who had never attached some deep sense to the notion of the Oracle within us—that ultimate ground and foundation of our moral being. No argument can be sound that has not that internal perception for its basis. All the rest may be accommodated to circumstances and expediency. Slavery has nothing to fear from logic—but it trembles at the voice of moral indignation. Be sure that wheresoever this Gospel of human Emancipation shall be preached, your works on slavery will be a Memorial of you. I never read any moral production that so filled my soul."*

My relief, however, was only partial, for on turning to the documents I saw that within no limits of becoming time could I convey to you the images they give: if we had had a week's conference on Channing I should have gladly undertaken what may be seen of him in the mirrors of these two powerful instruments of vision. And you can resort to them for yourselves; and you will do so if there is any reality in your presence here. The Introduction in which Channing concentrates and reflects himself is less than ten pages of the one volume edition of his works; I wish every one of us knew those pages by heart: and the Correspondence, except for the time it might make you meditate, would be but a short evening's reading. But let us here take one look at Channing as unconsciously he images himself. He asks, "How is a man known? What differences one man from another?". And the answer is, "His *predominant*

---

* "Life of Blanco White," Vol. III. p. 298.

thoughts, the *predominant* feelings and ideas, which give their hue and impulse to the common actions of his mind." We have seen what was Channing's "predominant thought," "the master light of all his seeing," the spiritual relationship of himself and of every man to God. Hence the mighty monotone of his mind, like the monotone of the ocean, which souls that are not attuned to it may sometimes feel oppressive. Hence, from that one impulse and root-principle, all the directions of his spirit, all the soarings of his genius, where free to take their *natural* way; and hence his awful tones when he had to turn upon *unnatural*, unbrotherly wrong the light of the judgment-seat of God. The natural history of the religious action and development of his character is most instructive, for it is that of all those who have made the spiritual eras of the world. First, the devout Seeker in retirement, silently taking in the Divine light and strength; afterwards the Hero of faith and righteousness, standing out before men in the whole armour of God. There was an early time when he appeared as one absorbed in piety, a saintly mystic,—not yet a warrior for the Right, a good soldier of Jesus Christ on the battle-field of the world,—even as the youthful Christ himself retired within the divine secrets and recesses of his being, and pleaded for the time against disturbing relationships:—" What have I to do with you?" "Know ye not that I mnst be about my Father's business?" "Your time is always ready, my time is not yet come." According to the saying, that we retreat for the sake of a mightier spring,

Channing was embosoming himself in the Fatherhood of God, that, when his hour came, he might carry the whole impulse and faith of that alliance into the service and the brotherhood of man. It was Religion that inspired him for philanthropy, supplied his instruments, and put on his armour. He was aware of the 'solemn monotone of his spirit, of the return of his mind to a few great convictions. In no other way could he do justice to the necessity that was on him to plead *effectually* for God and man. Chalmers, who was like him in moral ardour, said that as a preacher to men as they were, there was only one figure of speech for which he had the smallest respect, and that was Reiteration. But Channing's reiteration is never rhetoric; it is ever a fresh stroke, one stroke more of unexhausted emotion; the pressing out of another drop of the life-blood of Truth; if he repeats, or seems to repeat, it is to lay bare more of the grounds that make conviction sure; and you are always made to feel that the sustained heat and passion of his words are from the force of the underlying Realities, and that there is the living Rock beneath you. In the Correspondence with Blanco White this earnestness is the feature of Channing that is seen most vividly, as they flash the light to one another. Nothing appals him, or makes him despair of mankind, where there is faithfulness to conviction. In the most frightful perversions of religious Belief, with their cruel practical consequences, he finds it "comforting to think that the horrible doctrines of persecution were really held," and that in the cruelty there was the terrible force of mistaken duty. He says "that there is an evil far more to be deplored than doctrinal errors, and that is the *unfaithfulness* of Christians to the light they have attained," and he eagerly wants to know " among what bodies of Christians there has seemed to be the greatest *fidelity* to their *convictions*, be those convictions just or not." Blanco White's answer is most catholic in spirit, whilst he lays his finger on what must be the most powerful source of religious fidelity, wherever it *really* exists. He says that he has "found great faithfulness in individuals of the most opposite views as to the points disputed among Christians," —but that "wherever the intellectual and moral being is penetrated with the great truth of God's paternity in regard to us, and so Conscience has become His Oracle and His representative, faithfulness is the fruit and the result."

Music has entered largely into to-night's celebration, whether with a knowledge, or with an instinct, of its suitableness. Channing himself says, "I am conscious of a power in music which I want words to describe. It touches chords, reaches depths in the soul which lie beyond all other influences, extends my consciousness, and has sometimes given me a pleasure which I may have found in nothing else. Nothing in my experience is more mysterious, more inexplicable. An instinct has always led men to transfer it to Heaven, and, I suspect, the Christian under its power has often attained to a singular consciousness of his immortality. Facts of this nature make me feel what an infinite mystery our nature is, and how little our books of science reveal it to us." The answer of Blanco White, who was himself a scientific musician, and an exquisite performer, though it only echoes Channing, is too instructive an echo to be suppressed. Writing in a state of suffering, he says, "The internal lyre, to borrow the language of Socrates, has been unstrung within me. Large sums of money have, in my opinion, been wasted on the Bridgewater Treatises; yet no one has thought of Music as a proof of the intelligence and goodness of the Deity, though the relations of the musical ear with the vibrating bodies are as fixed and regular as the motions of the planets. Add, that the laws by which music produces its wonders are superinduced above those of mere hearing—a system within a system—for the purpose of the purest pleasure."—At the same time, whether Music has exhausted its resources to-night in providing what is most appropriate to so solemn an occasion, and so great a memory, I am not a musician, and I shall not presume to say, and should deem it ungracious to inquire.—The feelings with which we desire to-night to cherish the memory and the abiding influence of Channing, find perfect expression in a few words from a letter of his to myself, after the death of Blanco White:—" The daily privilege of communion with a great and good mind is a daily light shed over our path. But we will not say that we have lost such friends, They live within us in sweet and tender remembrances. They live around us in the fruits of their holy labours. They live above us, and call us in the tones of a friendship which Heaven has refined, to strengthen our union with them by sharing their progress in truth and virtue.

Now, we do not wish this Celebration to evaporate in praise, which Channing does not want, and which will do good to no one,—and what he has here said we may apply to our own relations to himself. We cannot over-estimate the blessing of living under the influence, and even under the awe, of a great mind. May God have compassion upon those who do not know what this experience is, who never look up to a fellow being, or tread as on holy ground; who are always walking among their equals or their inferiors, and with no true standard by which to measure themselves, know not what they are! This is what we should most dread at the ordinary centres of human intercourse, the marts of the world. Our associates are only our fellows : we are all equals, and the level is not high. We are too little toned, or chastened, or it may be disturbed, made diffident, by the touch of genius, or rare insight, or vast knowledge, or exalted goodness, and life becomes monotonous and commonplace. With slight modifications we are but repetitions of one another. Societies like ours should seek to attract towards them great minds as God's most signal blessings to mankind. Centres of light, of intellectual elevation, of spiritual dignity and power are especially needed at the centres of material wellbeing. I do not mean the able and ready man; I do not mean the man who has read the magazines and knows the latest speculation, and can speak of it with an easy but an uninspiring tongue, and is himself a magazine, not a fountain. I mean the man who has a spring of power in himself, who is great in his own department, who makes us feel the difference between native force and mere information. If, naturally, and they are rare anywhere, we must have few such men amongst us, and at present no institutions devoted to the higher education to quicken such seeds as God may have sown in our midst, the next best thing to their living presence is a knowledge of their lives, familiarity with their thoughts and leading impulses, not merely to have read but to *know* the Books that preserve the life blood of a great spirit. We read too much, too loosely, as Channing himself complained, as Bishop Butler complained a hundred and sixty years ago, only to let thoughts *pass through us*, instead of enshrining them as our own familiar spirits. What would Channing do for us, if we had him now in our midst? He might teach us nothing, add nothing to our knowledge except of ourselves, but we should all throb to his touch. I think the new College for Liverpool would get a mighty start. Nor is there one cause in this community affecting the interests of humanity, of Education, of Temperance, of the Elevation of the Labouring Classes, of the dignity of Work, of War, of Peace, of the influence of Art, Poetry and Beauty, and the spirit of Christ, the Nation's Honour and the Nation's Literature, that would not be invigorated by his way of speaking of them, his way of looking at them. What gave him this force? Earnestness, a sense of responsibility, faith in his inspirations, which above all earthly instruments is the genius of the soul, and the irresistible sword of the Almighty. And, if we may not live in intercourse with a great spirit, we are yet not left to ourselves. Moral greatness is, after all, the simplest, the most transparent thing in the world; its wisdom is goodness; its inspiration singleness of eye; its most penetrating insight an undivided heart; its purest magnanimity childlike sincerity and trust. We have the same means of becoming intimate with a great Man of this order that we have of becoming intimate with a Greater than he; but it is a blessed help to be able to ascend by steps to the greatest of all; and if this our Celebration here to-night has any meaning in it, if it is not all emptiness and words, if we should not feel a shame at taking part in it, it means for all of us, but especially for the most susceptible, for the young, the aspiring, for those not yet stiffened into moulds, in whom the spiritual ore is fusile still, that Channing, through their sustained acquaintance with him, is henceforth to be not a name, but a great power in their lives. And should these be my last words to the younger minds amongst us, I am content for those last words to be, that, next to the New Testament, of all the writings I know, I think the writings of Channing are the most likely to keep them in the line of spiritual advancement, humble, progressive, free, open to every light that comes from God, constrained by love to be of Christ's spirit towards the least of his brethren.

The Rev. CHARLES BEARD said:—If Mr. Thom found himself in a difficulty, how must I feel after you have listened to a speech so exquisitely impressive in its personal reminiscences, and so widely reaching and so deeply penetrating in its statements of religious truth? And I am also in the further difficulty that I am conscious that the evening has already far advanced, and that the chairman would have done well to accept the offer which I made to him a moment ago, to cut me out of the programme, and to let you arrive at home in decent time. We are indeed in a perplexity, because this subject has been discussed again and again, as Mr. Thom has already said, and almost every possible aspect of it has already been laid before the public by speakers and writers with great opportunities of knowledge and great powers of expression. But two or three Sundays ago, whilst you were engaged in your ordinary morning worship, I made a pilgrimage to the grave of Theodore Parker, which lies in the Protestant cemetery at the gate of Florence. The violets shed their fragrance under my feet, the sad cypresses shot their green flames overhead, and all round about was the hum and the noise of that great and famous city over which Dante yearned, which Michael Angelo loved with all the passion of his soul, and which Savonarola awoke to brief repentance from its sins. And it has struck me since that it would be possible to give some little novelty to the treatment of the subject which is asked of me to-night, if I were to venture for a few moments upon a parallel between those two great souls which it was the fortune of Boston—not a very considerable city in point of population—to produce within a very few years of one another. Because, however, their differences have been exaggerated by partisan feeling on either side, there can be no doubt whatever to any one who looks at their life and writings from some little distance of time, and from an impartial point of criticism, that they were one in far more than they were two; that Parker would never have been possible without Channing, and that one of the facts of Channing's life which we reflect upon with the greatest pleasure is that at the moment of the crisis of Parker's fate he said, " Give my love to Mr. Parker, and tell him to speak out his whole heart." Now, I said in the first place that Parker would not have been possible without Channing. Where, except from Channing, did he derive that boundless faith in human nature which was so strongly characteristic of the older preacher? Where, but from Channing, did he derive that intensely moral conception of the nature of religion, and especially of the nature of Christianity? You do not find these things in old-fashioned New England Presbyterianism, you don't find them in the school of thought which prevailed both in England and America at the close of the eighteenth Century. Channing was in America, and to a large extent in England too, himself the point of transition between them, and it was at the feet of Channing, whether Parker knew it or not, that he learned much that made him afterwards the pure and fervent and powerful soul that he was. I know nothing so shameful in the whole history of religious persecution, as the persecution which was raised against Parker for his discourse "On the Transient and Permanent in Christianity." There have been persecutions which have raged more fiercely against men's bodies, persecutions whose instruments were the axe, the faggot, and the thumb-screw, but the particular iniquity in this persecution was that it was excited by men who themselves were brand-marked with heresy, and whose only allegation against Parker was that, in the exercise of his freethought he had gone a little further than themselves. Mr. Bright has already said, and we all know very well, that Channing's views of Christianity were not Parker's. We know that Parker said many things, especially in the latter part of his life, which Channing perhaps would have heard with unwilling ears, but you will never make me believe that the older prophet did not know what he was doing when he sent that loving message to the younger—you will never make me think that he did not feel that he was standing upon the verge of a new era, and that he looked out upon it with a full confidence that, come what might, his landmarks of religion were of a kind that could neither be submerged nor removed, and that God would still be holy, and human nature worthy, and Christ the leading light of humanity, whatever might be the result of criticism. Now, I suppose these two great men were equally distinguished by the love of truth—it is a marked characteristic of all prophetic souls—and I should hesitate to say which of them loved truth the most faithfully. But they sought truth in very different ways. I do not know whether Parker was a great scholar. I do know that he was a great and omnivorous reader, and a mighty collector of books. His writings often bristle with quotations from all manner of recondite authors; but when you come to Channing's writings you find no quotations at all. Whatever learning he had was so amalgamated with himself, so assimilated to the texture of his mind, that it seemed only to feed the natural fountain of thought as it flowed out of his pure soul. And whereas the one man was a wanderer in intellectual regions, a bee sucking honey from "every flower that grows," so the other was a quiet meditative soul, rarely venturing beyond the precincts of his own study or summer retreat, and letting truth, as it shone upon him from every quarter of the heavens, find its way silently and thoughtfully into his mind. And again, as one man spoke hotly, passionately—had a word in every controversy—looked forward to the execution of large intellectual and literary schemes, so it was characteristic of the other to say nothing except upon emergency, to keep his best work for the pulpit, and when he spoke, as he sometimes felt himself compelled to speak, upon other topics, and address the literary world in the United States and in this country—he allowed his thoughts to come from him almost without care for what might become of them. Parker and Channing addressed a very different order of minds. They were both of them, I believe, in the essential sense of the words, mystics, that is to say, they were men who had the vision and the faculty divine, and who looked in God's face and spoke of what they saw. They were both of them men of deep individuality; but Channing spoke or speaks, to a very large extent, to men who have been under the influence of orthodox views—and who are about to shake them off in the force of a moral impulse—whilst Parker is the guide of those venturesome souls who are always voyaging away into the sunny seas of the unknown, hardly caring, perhaps, in what harbour they ultimately arrive. And yet both of them were ardent servants of the truth, and both of them ready, if need be, to lay down their lives for truth. It is, again, a characteristic difference between the two men that, while they were both ardent lovers of Christ, they loved him, as it were, with a different species of affection. Channing, who was almost of age when the nineteenth century began, and who therefore had got his first training in the very different school of thought which prevailed in the last century—was never much disturbed by modern criticism and was content to take the Scriptures as he got them. Parker, on the contrary, was one of the men who welcomed every new theory as it came from Germany— to whom nothing came amiss that any man said or thought. And whilst to Channing Christ was a being above humanity—the Son of God made flesh, the image of the Father's grace and truth, one in whom, he felt, was united everything that was best in humanity, or reflected it in its highest degree, one to whom he looked to be the inspiring strength of mankind in future ages; a bright and beautiful Being, yet no vision indeed, but a heavenly reality—to Parker, who hardly loved Christ less, if less at all, He was the carpenter's son, a man who had gone about the villages of Galilee, not knowing where to lay his head; one who had mingled with the common people. One might almost say that

he loved Him better if he could feel that he was in truth
a man like ourselves, one born in the midst of us, owning
our weaknesses, and exhibiting our possible strength.
And yet I would not say that the one man loved his
master less than the other. I do not know where you
would go for stronger, more devout, more affectionate
expression of love to the great Galilean prophet than
you can find in Parker's works. So that while they both
loved Christ, they loved him in a different fashion. I
cannot, in thus speaking of these two men, do more
than allude to their relation to the moral controversies
of their time. They were both men who felt as such
men must feel, in the very depths of their nature, the
iniquity of negro slavery; but while it was the characteristic
of Channing that he could only speak well-balanced
words, even if they were words of reprobation, and
that he must seek out precisely the right time to speak,
and choose the very words and no others which would
aptly express and weigh both sides of the question,
Parker went down into the throng of men, worked upon
committees, helped to incite rebellion, took the fugitive
slave to his own house, and braved the penalties of the law,
—aye, and more than once looked up at the muskets
that hung in his study, and which his ancestors had carried
at Lexington, and wondered whether he would have to
take them down and use them in the cause of human liberty.
So whilst on the one side there was something shrill
and almost passionate in Parker's rebuke of public wrong,
on the other side, men said that Channing did not speak
soon enough, and spoke too softly when he did speak.

Parker's voice was like a trumpet that was perpetually sounding in the midst of men—shrill and clear, demanding instant attention to whatever he had to say. Channing's like the solemn note of an organ, filling the air with the sweet, strong utterance of eternal principles of right. I do not know whether Parker was a very strong man, but he had within him that spring of energy which some men possess, and which enables weak natures to do the work of strong ones, and he killed himself by overwork. And Channing was essentially a delicate man—a man who had to spare himself—who could only speak now and then. He was obliged to reserve himself for great occasions: he could not do even his pulpit work without long intervals of rest; but when he did speak it was just as if the words fell from Heaven upon Boston. That a man so far removed from ordinary business and common passions, should yet speak so strong words for right, made Channing's soft accents as powerful as Parker's passionate utterance. Whilst Channing sleeps amongst his own people at Auburn, Parker's remains lie under the cypresses at Florence. But the words of the old Latin maxim are true, "*Omne solum forti patria,*"—every country is the brave man's home; and certainly every country finds a fit grave for a brave man. If it is well that Channing should sleep with his own people, it is not less well that Parker should lie at Florence beneath the tower of Giotto, and the dome of Brunelleschi: where Michael Angelo and Galileo lie; and—better than all—where Savonarola preached and suffered.

And who is there to take up the torch that Channing handed to Parker: that Parker let drop from his dying hand at Florence? Not one of us is fit for so great a trust. We have heard to day that this is the birthday of our own living prophet, who though he has ended his third quarter of a century, still, we rejoice to know, has his eye yet undimmed, and his natural force not abated. Perhaps there may be some boy growing up amongst us who will add something of Channing's saintness, something of Parker's fervour to the beautiful philosophical spirit of the prophet whom we have yet amongst us. One thing I know, truth will never lack a servant, God will never be without worthy children, nor is the church in time to come, as in time past, likely ever to be barren of saints.

The Rev. WILLIAM BINNS said:—There are eight Roman Catholic saints whose memories are celebrated on Channing's birthday, and, putting his theology on one side, and looking at the spirit of his life, there are many Roman Catholics who would willingly accept him as a ninth; and perhaps a liberal Pope, as the development of doctrine proceeds, may some time canonize him, notwithstanding his theology. The Positivists certainly ought to give Channing a place in their calendar. He has a better right to be there than many mere warriors who figure prominently in it, and than some mythological personages, such as Prometheus, Hercules, and Orpheus, whose very existence is a fable of the poets. Channing illustrated Comte's service of humanity without falling into Comte's extravagance of ignoring God, and I would recommend the Liverpool Positivist Society to atone for the deficiency of their master, and to set apart the 7th of April or the 13th of Archimedes for Channing. Diophantus possesses that day already, and I have no objection to let him remain. Among the multitudes who claim the 7th of April as their birthday, as well as Channing, there are three who have a near spiritual kinship to him : Wordsworth, who represents the higher religious aspirations of Channing in moods when Wordsworth is as little of a sectarian Anglican as Channing is a sectarian Unitarian ; St. Francis Xavier, for Francis Xavier was a true saint, if the world ever had one, who represents Channing's practical Christian enthusiasm ; and Fourier, the French philosophical Socialist, who represents, though in a form of chaotic and misdirected science, Channing's longings for a Utopian condition of society. If Canon Farrar had been appointed to the bishopric of Liverpool—I mean the bishopric of the second order, for the bishopric of the first order naturally belongs to the older church—he would have made some of the characteristics of the Channing theology immensely popular. But, unhappily for him, and unhappily for the religious life of the town, the publication of " Eternal Hope " made his prospects hopeless. If he had vaguely hinted at his sublime and beautiful heresies, and not plainly stated them, we might have had him here instead of Dean Ryle, and perhaps with us to-night. Channing's sociology came, as everything good in every man's case generally does come, out of his religion. Now, Channing's fundamental religious ideas were three—first, God is perfect; second, Jesus Christ is the true type of a man after God's own heart; and third, in universal human nature there are the germs of this true type of a man after God's own heart. I am content for to-night to take my stand on them. The additions that Channing made, and the additions that are made by the compilers of and believers in elaborate confessions of faith, I pass by as not needed for myself, and as destined to be gradually eliminated by the course of history, serving a purpose while they last, but still being a slowly dying cause. Christian manhood then—and I include, of course, womanhood in manhood—is the end and aim for which social institutions are established. This is their *raison d'être*; we preserve them as they promote it, we discard them as they hinder it, and we modify them as we get clearer views of what is required by the ever-unfolding capacities of mankind. In the animating spirit of these ideas Channing bravely faced the problems of the time. To begin with, they made short work of his early Calvinism, and emancipated him into the glorious liberty of the children of God. With the various social activities that they prompted him to undertake I find myself substantially at one, and with the political activities too, for politics is but a minor section of the larger sphere of sociology. So he condemned slavery in days when all the respectabilities defended it, and when all the pieties, except honest

Quaker piety, said, "Let it alone." It always seems to me a melancholy thing, and an illustration of the perverting influence which the possession of irresponsible, absolute power exercises over the conscience and the conduct of even good men, that the American people, while asserting their own liberty, and shedding their blood in lavish streams to win it, did not sooner realize that in an equitable government fashioned after divine models, liberty is just as much the birthright of the blacks as of the whites. They, however, took refuge in a policy of short-sighted utilitarianism. I say shortsighted, because in the long run utilitarianism ends in morality which does right for right's sake, and does not consider utility; utility goes without the saying, righteousness is the guarantee of the only utility worth caring for. Channing did not live to see the triumph of his principles. That triumph had to be achieved by war. It was evolved as a providential consequence of mixed human purposes. Liberty is an inspired saying. But the Americans found out the truth of Tennyson's words that it is—

> "A saying hard to shape in act;
> For all the past of time reveals
> A bridal dawn of thunder peals
> Whenever thought has wedded fact."

The American thunder peals purified the air and set the people free. Channing was a Republican, and hereditary privileges were alien to his generous and freedom-loving soul. In England we are not as yet, except in a few cases, educated up to the level of this lofty ideal of statesmanship. His political doctrines, therefore, run counter to some of our prejudices, and I should not have mentioned them if justice to him would have allowed me to keep silence. But we want to grasp him in his completeness, and this republicanism is an essential element of his sociology. For practical purposes we no doubt possess most of the advantages of republicanism, and it may be that our nearly real republicanism works about as well as the nominal combined with the real republicanism of America works. But old forms unfortunately tend now and then to reassert themselves as living forces. That is their nature. And I look upon Channing as a prophet of the good time coming, when effete forms also will disappear; when there will be no hereditary privileges; when the position of men and women will be determined by what they are, and not fixed beforehand by what their parents were, irrespective of their own present fitness; when, in simple parlance, every tub will stand on its own bottom. There is no need to hurry any changes in England. But it is evident that the social organism is working its way onward by natural and inevitable processes of development, and the future will be republican. Channing was a peace man, not a peace at any price man, for he believed, and I believe, in war sometimes as a bitter necessity—war for justice, war for liberty, war for the right to live and grow to the full stature of humanity, and death before slavery and dishonour. I have no inclination to abandon the world to the dominion of strong wickedness; the tender mercies of the wicked are cruel. I hold with Milton that a man must be willing to defend his country with the pen or the sword, as need may be. And—

> "How can a man die better than facing fearful odds
> For the ashes of his fathers and the temples of his gods?"

But notwithstanding this warlike preamble, I too am a peace man, and I candidly confess that I do not know of a single war in which we have been engaged, since the defeat of the Spanish Armada, which might not have been avoided by wise and Christian statesmanship, by a display of that scientific diplomacy of which we hear so much and see so little. England has still more faith in power than in righteousness, and is too ready to appeal to the arbitrament of arms instead of the arbitrament of the conscience of the world, and to show at the same time there is power enough at the back which we will call into play when peaceful proposals, pressed with an almost but not quite everlasting patience, have failed. A general reduction of armies and navies, a discouragement of the war spirit, a ceasing to confer honours on the fighting ruffian athletes of the Lord William Beresford stamp, the establishment of courts of international arbitration, whose decisions shall be enforced by the omnipotent international power—this was Channing's ideal, and to this the peoples will yet bring their governments. God grant it may be soon; it is weary waiting. Channing believed in free churches. So do most of us. Else wherefore are we here? "An Established Church," said he, "is the grave of intellect." And I see no possibility of answering that statement satisfactorily. The Church of England itself furnishes at once the best and the saddest commentary that we could desire. I admit with glad gratitude the number of eminent men who have adorned it. I remember Anselm's acute metaphysical intellect; I remember Jeremy Taylor, the Shakspeare of divines; I remember Hooker, with his ecclesiastical polity so much broader than Cartwright's Puritan scheme; I remember Tillotson's latitudinarianism; I remember Bishop Butler, with the "Analogy of Religion," so splendid in its first part and so halting in its second; I remember Dean Stanley, with his all-embracing geniality and charity—I remember them all, and whether I agree with them or disagree with them, I am proud of them. But they have one drawback, and in my mind that hampers and mutilates them from Anslem to Dean Stanley, hampers and mutilates the laity as well as the clergy. They are not free. Their thinking is bound to reach certain conclusions. Or, if they reach conclusions not in harmony with the plain meaning of the standards, they must either play tricks with words or seek a new home; and I feel, therefore, that if, when limited by creeds, they are able to do so well, they would be able to do vastly better if they threw their creeds simply to fly in the winds as temporary flags, and did not inscribe upon them an inglorious *semper eadem*. Now, Channing would not have his own creed established, nor would we have ours so doomed to be stereotyped. Let theology be as science is, open to new revelations; and let it throw aside old forms and old symbols of speech, as it presses into an ampler ether and a diviner air. And to this complexion, too, England, will come at last. Channing believed in woman. So, again, do we all. But there are three ways of believing in woman. We may believe in her as a creature made for us to hold as a chattel, which belief we have outgrown; or as a creature to be protected and cared for by the superior lords of creation, which belief is still the prevailing superstition; or as a creature not only to be protected and cared for, but possessing the same rights as ourselves to the full development of all her natural faculties, which belief some of us have attained, and more vaguely sympathize with, and all are destined to. This last form of belief was Channing's. What does it involve? It involves a higher education of women, and by means of high schools and an extension of university opportunities we are slowly moving in the right direction. But when we have given a higher education to woman there will be little use in it, it will simply rust in her if we do not frankly open to her the various professions. And here men, in spite of their politeness, are often tyrannical, jealous, and selfish. Doctors protest, lawyers protest, parsons protest this, that, and the other is not her sphere. I protest in my turn against them all. Let woman choose her own sphere. She cannot make a greater mess of things than many male doctors, lawyers, and parsons make already, and the chances are that she would often do very much better. And, to crown all, give her the legal right to the franchise, and to more control over the joint property and the personal property, and so, in harmony with Channing's ideal, though I do not know that he ever formulated it in this way, bring law up to the demands of morality. This revolution will come to pass also. Finally, Channing believed in the elevation of the social condition of the working classes. He sympathized with some of the ends that Fourier and Robert Owen set before themselves. He did not, of course, sanction Fourier's mechanical arrangements, and still less did he fall in with Owen's parallelograms and community of property and doctrine of circumstances. But he felt the startling anomaly in a Christian country of so many poor in the face of a handful of the rich. America, to its discredit, has no poor laws. Channing insisted that it was the duty of a State to care for its poorer citizens, to educate them, and to protect them in sickness and old age. He constantly urged on the rich their moral obligations in this matter, and was prepared to make sweeping reforms of a legal kind in relation to land and other property. But, and what is always of supreme importance, he clearly saw that no laws, no elaborate, artificial, social arrangements could of themselves destroy our social evils. Only to the elevation of the personal character can we look for the permanent elevation of the whole social system. Temperance, industry, economy, self-control, morality, religion, are the genuine levers to raise humanity. He was a socialist, but he preserved the sanctity of the individual and the home, and made personal and family life the basis of national prosperity and social progress. There is one aspect of Channing's theology on which I must say a concluding word. He has exercised a wide and healthy influence over the old-fashioned methods of theological thinking, and that influence is still growing from year to year. Perhaps it is owing less to his power as a thinker, than to his moral and spiritual earnestness as a man. It was also moral and spiritual earnestness that made him a heretic himself to begin with, and compelled him in very fidelity to his own best instincts to believe in a potential divinity of human nature in spite of its waywardness and sin, and to re-interpret the work of Christ as a quickening agency rather than a legal satisfaction, and to assert the ultimate victory of God in harmony with the freedom of God's children, over against the prevailing notion of a disastrous and deplorable break-down, in which the devil, and not God, gets the better in the great conflict between good and evil. And Channing's ideas on these matters now find multitudinous expression in the Pulpit and the Press on the part of men who differ from him on the Trinity, and still cling to the Incarnation as the cardinal truth of Christianity. But he has weaned them from the idolatry of creeds, and they no longer, to anything like the same extent, hold that their own little cluster of dogmas constitutes the sole way to heaven. They gladly reckon themselves members of a universal church, and the ancient anathemas, that consistency seems to require, they only utter from the lips outward, and take care to explain the meaning away. Channing's unique spiritual personality has made a breach in the citadel of bigotry. Through him we can see rising in the midst of the erst orthodox world a new temple for a new faith, lofty as is the love of God, and ample as the wants of man. I have now, from my own standpoint, briefly sketched some of the phases of Channing's manifold activity. You may not agree with all the details of his views; but, like me, I am sure that you will bow before his spirit. I say that as a free and catholic religionist, as an enemy of slavery, as a republican, as a friend of peace, as a believer in free churches, as an advocate of the equal rights of man and woman, as a servant of God and the people, he was a hero in his own country and a saint worthy of the worship of mankind.

Mr. C. T. BOWRING proposed the following resolution:—"That the best thanks of this meeting be given to the Rev. J. H. Thom, the Rev. Charles Beard, and the Rev. W. Binns for their interesting addresses." He was sure that a deep interest was felt in the occasion that had brought them there that night, and that interest must be very much increased and heightened by the pleasure it gave them to see their venerable friend Mr. Thom present. They had listened to his address with very great pleasure, and he hoped that he might be spared many years to again appear amongst them.

The CHAIRMAN, in putting the resolution, said it was a wise saying of the great Italian poet that when they had reached the middle stage of life, it was a good thing for them to pause awhile amid the dust and turmoil of their daily lives, and, casting an earnest gaze upon the years that they had passed, endeavour earnestly to gather from them lessons of wisdom and elements of strength with which to meet effectually the exigencies that they might be called to meet in the years that might be in store for them. In like manner, that night, he was sure that they would all feel that it had been good for them to turn their thoughts away for a moment from the contemporaneous lives around them, and under such able guidance as that of the three gentlemen who had addressed them turn their earnest gaze upon the past lifework of such a man as Channing, who, without any advantages, by the force of his solemn conviction and his earnest feeling, moulded the thoughts of the present age in the direction of freedom. He had no doubt that they would all join gladly in offering their earnest thanks to those gentlemen who had so nobly taken their thoughts backwards upon this life.

Upon the motion of Mr. HENRY JEVONS, a vote of thanks was passed to the chairman, and the proceedings afterwards terminated.

ARTICLES AND NOTICES.

The Christian World, March, 28th, 1880.

Dr. CHANNING combined in his character so many qualities that were great and noble, and, therefore, worthy to be mentioned for stimulus and example, that it is difficult to indicate them in the brief space available for the purpose. We should say that the two crowning qualities of his nature which can never be forgotten, even in the slightest measure, when we think of him, were his *intense consciousness of God*, and his *deep reverence for humanity*. It would be easy to show that there were many other qualities which, in the degree in which he possessed and developed them, would have sufficed to make a great reputation; but of these it is not necessary to speak. Channing seems to us colossal in his greatness when we remember his reverence for God, and his marvellous respect for man. One can hardly help saying, that if men could only share ever so faintly his conception of God, they could not help fearing and loving Him. The Divine Father was a different Being in his view from what He is to multitudes of our race, who yet consider themselves to be religious, and are so considered by their fellow-men. "Intimate and tender," said he, "beyond our highest conception, is our Heavenly Father's relationship to us. How near to me is my Creator! I am not merely surrounded by His influence, as by this air which I breathe. I am pervaded by His agency; He quickens my whole being. Through Him am I this instant thinking, feeling, and speaking; and knowing thus the intensity and extent of this relationship, how is it possible that I can forget Him?" It is not wonderful that one who believed in God thus, should say, that "the light of life is a constant consciousness of Divine fellowship." No wonder that with so much doctrinal interpretation of the Divine character abounding on all sides of him, he should have asked, "Is God seen to be a PARENT? Is not the intercourse with him too formal? Do we not need an exhibition of his near relationship to us which will awaken a stimulating, filial, rejoicing, confiding piety? Do we *believe* that he loves us *infinitely*, that a stream of goodness is for ever flowing down upon us, that He delights in forgiving, that He joyfully welcomes His returning children? Is this the great view to be presented, that God is desirous to impart *Himself* to us, to unite us to Him in perfect love? Any view of God of which love is not the centre is injurious to the soul which receives it." Channing yearned for a wider prevalence of such views as these concerning the Deity; and although we are living in a day which has welcomed them more heartily than the times gone by, we must not forget that Channing was one of the earliest of that small, but noble band which did its utmost to give them expression and currency in the world. A generation or two before Dean Mansel had written his treatise on "The Limits of Religious Thought," and his vigorous opponents—John Stuart Mill of the number—had raised their protests against the notion that the morality of God might be different from that of man—Channing had written in a review, on "The Moral Argument Against Calvinism:" "We maintain that God's attributes are intelligible, and that we can conceive as truly of His goodness and justice as of those qualities in man; in fact, these qualities are essentially the same in God and man. They differ in degree, in purity, and in extent of operation. We know not, and we cannot conceive of any other justice or goodness than we learn from our nature; and if God have not these, He is altogether unknown to us as a moral Being. He offers nothing for esteem and love to rest upon; the objection of the infidel, is just, that worship is wasted—'we worship we know not what.'" The character of the Divine Being was so darkly and sternly represented in times gone by (yet not so distant but that some who are living now can remember them), that we can hardly compute our obligations to good and noble men like Channing, who rubbed away the dust and dirt with which the portraiture of God had been covered by the neglect, the misuse, and the *bad varnish* of both priests and presbyters in the previous ages. "God is our Father," said Channing, "not merely because He created us, or because He gives us enjoyment, for He created the flower and the insect, yet we call Him not their Father: this bond is a spiritual one, this name belongs to God because He frames spirits like Himself, and delights to give them what is most glorious and blessed in His own nature." He regarded the revelation in the New Testament of the Fatherhood of God, as the brightest feature of that book which could be named. The man's whole soul was in his words when he said, "Without God our existence has no support, our life no aim, our improvements no permanence, our best labours no sure and enduring results, our spiritual weakness no power to lean upon, and our noblest aspirations and desires no pledge of being realized in a better state. Struggling virtue has no friend, suffering virtue no promise of victory. Take away God, and life becomes mean, and man poorer than the brute."

It was just because Channing realized with so much intensity the greatness of the Divine glory in its moral aspects and relations, that he came to hold the views which he has expressed in unnumbered sermons concerning the dignity of human nature. "I am accustomed," he said, "to speak of the greatness of human nature, but it is great only through its parentage; great, because descended from God, because connected with a goodness and power with which it is to be enriched for ever; and nothing but the consciousness of this connection can give that hope of elevation through which alone the mind is to rise to true strength and liberty." Many years ago a young minister of our acquaintance in the earliest days of his ministerial work, when visiting a family in the congregation, had the door opened to him by a servant, whom he recognized as a "member in society." The young minister was certainly not of a haughty disposition, but he was not a little astonished, and just a little ruffled, when this servant put forth her hand to shake his own. He mentioned it to the colleague with whom he was working. The good man said "Why not, my brother; why not?" and asked him if he had read Dr. Channing's sermons upon "Honour due to all men." Fetching it from a shelf in his study, he handed it to the young minister, who thus for the first time made its acquaintance. It was read with solid delight, and not only led him to an acquaintance with Channing's works, for which he has been deeply grateful, but produced an abiding impression upon his character. In this sermon it is, that Channing says, "Nothing is to make man a true lover of man but the discovery of something interesting and great in human nature." "I have no desire," he says, "to derogate from the honour paid to great men, but I say, let them not rise by the depression of the multitude." "I see men," he observes, "placed by their Creator, on a field of battle, but compassed with peril that they may triumph over it; and though often overborne, still summoned to new efforts, still privileged to approach the Source of all power, and to seek 'grace in time of need;' and still addressed in tones of encouragement by a celestial Leader who has Himself fought and conquered, and holds forth to them His own Crown of righteousness and victory." He shows in this sermon, as elsewhere, that in honouring human nature, the true principle of all good education takes its rise, and also of all benevolent enterprises on behalf of the poor. "A fraternal union founded on this deep conviction, and intended to lift up and strengthen the exposed and tempted poor, is to do infinitely more for that suffering class than all our artificial associations; and till Christianity shall have breathed into us the spirit of respect for our nature, wherever it is found, we shall do them little good." In his lectures on the "Elevation of the Labouring Portion of the Community," he indicates broadly and strongly the true foundation of the principal sentiments by which men should be actuated. "Man," he observes, "is a free being: created to act from a spring in his own breast, to form himself, and to decide his own destiny; connected intimately with nature, but not enslaved to it; connected still more closely with God, yet not enslaved even to the Divinity, but having power to render or withhold the service due to his Creator; encompassed by a thousand warring forces, by physical elements which inflict pleasure and pain, by dangers seen and unseen; by the influences of a tempting, sinful world; yet endued by God with power to contend with all; to perfect himself by conflict with the very forces which threaten to overwhelm him. Such is the idea of man." It will be clear to the reader who ponders these words, that Channing must of necessity have become an earnest friend of education, anti-slavery movements, and all efforts which had for their object the elevation of mankind and the glory of God. Such, indeed, he was. And since his speech and his writings drew their inspiration from sources far within his soul, we are not surprised that Longfellow said of him in the month of Channing's death, before he had even heard of that event—

> " The pages of thy book I read,
>   And as I closed each one,
> My heart responding, ever said,
>   ' Servant of God, well done ! '
>
> " Well done ! thy words are great and bold ;
>   At times they seem to me
> Like Luther's in the days of old,
>   Half *battles* for the free."

It is surely fitting, in review of the exceeding service rendered by this good man to the cause of humanity and spiritual religion, that his birthday should be remembered with thankful joy by all who are seeking to do honour to humanity, and to bring glory to the great Father of all.

Pall Mall Gazette, April 7th, 1880.

THE hundredth anniversary of the birth of Channing will be celebrated this evening in public meetings by a large number of people in the United States, and by a considerable number even in England. Celebrations of this kind are as a rule very unwisely conducted ; but as Channing's admirers belong to a well educated class, it may be assumed that most of the speeches in his honour will be marked by intelligence and good taste. He is known in this country mainly as the representative of American Unitarianism, but he himself disliked to be closely identified with any particular sect. He was willing to be called a Unitarian, he somewhere says, merely because the name was to some extent one of reproach. One of his leading ideas, indeed, was that sects have, on the whole, exerted a pernicious influence. In nearly all his religious discourses he gives expression to this conviction, insisting that his readers must not regard his opinions as more than the conclusions of a solitary thinker, and that if they wish to arrive at a decision on the questions he discusses they are bound to investigate the evidence for themselves. And he placed no limits on the freedom of criticism. Every belief, no matter how it might be sanctioned by tradition, was to be examined afresh in the light of modern knowledge, and doctrines for which no adequate foundation could be discovered were to be fearlessly abandoned. In this teaching Channing was, of course, simply a consistent Protestant, carrying the principles of the Reformation to their legitimate conclusion; but at the time when he began his public career it was teaching which had hardly obtained a hearing in the United States. Until about the beginning of the present century the religion which dominated the American people was the narrowest form of Puritanism. Departure from the system of Calvin was considered to be not so much of a mistake as a crime, and heretics were visited with the heaviest social penalties. The inevitable consequence was almost complete intellectual stagnation. Men of talent were afraid to enter upon inquiries which might lead to inconvenient results, and in every department of thought ignored facts and arguments that seemed even in a remote degree to conflict with accepted dogmas. Channing did essential service to his country by casting discredit on this intolerant temper. He was not the first American who spoke clearly and strongly in favour of free investigation, but he was the first to do so in a manner which attracted general attention, and which commanded the respect of the most thoughtful section of the community. He had too little of the historic spirit to understand that every phase of serious religious belief has corresponded to real necessities of human nature at particular stages of development, but his love of liberty made him remarkably fair in his treatment of opinions with which he himself did not agree. American Protestants were astonished to learn that in his view Catholicism was not simply a monstrous system of superstition. He even insisted that the Catholic Church has a much better right than any Protestant sect to claim infallibility; and in his admirable essay on Fenelon he took occasion to show that under certain conditions it is capable of producing very rare and beautiful types of character. There are indications that he could also appreciate some aspects of the great Oriental religions. To Calvinism alone he was a little unjust, but this was perhaps to be expected from the peculiar nature of what Mr. Spencer would call his " environment."

Channing made sincere and persistent attempts to reconsider the problems of religious philosophy, but it cannot be said that his efforts were attended with much success. He eliminated from the popular conception of Christianity everything that offended his reason and moral sense; but he retained those miraculous elements which have formed the chief difficulty of modern criticism. In holding this position he either went too far or did not go far enough. If we accept a miraculous system we are bound to believe that it has been introduced into the world for some adequate reason; it must be associated with a body of doctrine to which the human mind would not have risen by its own unaided powers. What Channing called Christianity cannot possibly be regarded as a body of doctrine of this nature; it was made up of a few beliefs which may easily be held without supernatural sanctions. And we may add that it has much less power to move the common mass of men than the so-called orthodox creed in almost any of its shapes. Unitarians dilate in vain on the superiority of a purely spiritual faith, for, although they may appeal with effect to a limited class, ordinary people are untouched by truths which are incapable of sensuous representation. Grillparzer has said that "religion is the poetry of unpoetical natures." Without taking this epigram too seriously, we may at any rate confidently assert that a religion cannot be popular which does not possess poetical qualities; and there are, unquestionably, poetical qualities (of a kind) in the ideas not only of Catholicism but even of despised

Calvinism. Channing's answer would be that these ideas are incredible; but it is an obvious retort that if a man is prepared to accept miracles he may without much hesitation accept a great deal more. "Dans cette voie," says M. Renan, "il n'y a que le premier pas qui coûte." In dealing with the question of miracles Channing failed to perceive the character which the controversy had assumed even in his day. He knew too little of physical science to understand the full force of the objection drawn from the uniformity of nature; and he did not give sufficient attention to the great critical movement in Germany which began with Lessing, and found its most important representatives in Strauss and the Tübingen school. The same lack of adequate thought and research may be detected in his treatment of subjects still more fundamental than those directly relating to miracles. Since the dawn of modern philosophy the constant tendency of theism has been to merge in pantheism. Channing had an occasional glimpse of this fact, but he never grasped its significance. It did not occur to him to inquire how far the tendency was justified, or whether it had any bearing on his favourite doctrines of free-will and immortality.

In his essay on Milton he suggests that it is not well for a thinker to be greatly in advance of his epoch; and the remark may perhaps be applied to his own case. By his comparative moderation he conciliated classes who would have bitterly opposed a more logical writer, while his opinions diverged sufficiently from received standards to stimulate independent reflection. His style exactly corresponded to the character of his thought. He indulged in none of those large phrases by which some later American writers have sought to give an appearance of novelty to old ideas, nor did he ever aim at the kind of "subtle" effects which are at present so much in favour. He contented himself for the most part with plain, straightforward language; yet there is hardly a dull line in his writings. Everywhere he impresses his readers with a sense of his sincerity and earnestness, and sometimes, when his feelings are strongly moved, he rises to a height of calm and impressive eloquence. It was not, however, merely as a writer that he benefited America; during the whole of his public career he acted as a philanthropist of the truest stamp. Slavery had no more vigorous or resolute enemy, although he opposed it without giving offence to the better class of slave-owners; and there was hardly a movement for the elevation of the working classes which he did not energetically support. In an able but rather patronising article on Channing, M. Renan talks as if there was no place in his ideal of a cultivated community for the elements which give variety and grace to educated European society. This is to do great injustice to a man of comprehensive and enlightened sympathies. Channing was a democrat by conviction as well as by birth, but the democracy to which he looked forward was one which would know how to appreciate art and literature, and which would respect individuality of character. Whether such a democracy is possible may be open to question; but there can be no doubt as to his conviction that this alone would be a worthy future for his country. And he seems never to have doubted that the object, great and difficult as it is, would ultimately be attained. He was a born optimist, and took continual pleasure in noting what he supposed to be signs of rapid social growth. His optimism was partly the result of keeping in the background half the facts of life, but it was perhaps a healthier mood than the despair of progress which has seized so many fine minds all over the civilized world in the second half of the nineteenth century. At any rate, it had an excellent effect on Channing, for he was one of the most cheerful as well as one of the most useful men of his day. When asked a few months before his death what he considered the happiest period of life, he answered with a smile, "About sixty."

Daily Telegraph, April 7th, 1880.

To-day is celebrated the centenary of a great and good man, William Ellery Channing, of Boston. One hundred years is long enough to enable the world to forget anybody, unless indeed he be of that illustrious band whose life-work can never be an anachronism. That a writer, or teacher, or leader of his fellows should survive in the popular memory for the lapse of a century is a strong test of the lasting worth of what he has done in and for the world; and that William Ellery Channing's career has stood that test must be most gratifying to all who have an abiding faith in the ultimate equity of popular appreciations. His festival is now being celebrated by the people of his own country, and there are some reasons why it ought not to be forgotten by the people of England as well. Dr. Channing was one of the great leaders of opinion, we might even say he was one of the great formers of thought, on the American continent, having the settled conviction that the cause of human progress mainly depended on the friendly relations of Britain and the United States being strengthened and not weakened. That is a common enough notion now, but in Dr. Channing's younger days it was only too fashionable both in this country and among our kin across the sea, to act and talk as though the eternal necessities of the universe had decreed that England and America must ever be deadly enemies. For those who, like Channing, set themselves to dispel this extraordinary and pernicious delusion, we who are enjoying the result of their labours ought to have even more than a passing word of homage to spare, and more than a passing thought may well be devoted to the salient points in the career of one who, like Leigh Hunt's sage, might have said of himself, "Write me as one who loved his fellow men." Like most leaders of opinion in a serious and highly-educated commonwealth, Dr. Channing was a clergyman; but it is not as the apostle of modern Unitarianism that we desire to direct attention to his life. Though a formidable polemic, he disliked ecclesiastical controversy, and if he did more than any man of his age to popularise the doctrines of his creed, we must admit that it was because he was usually the attacked and not the attacking party that his theology sometimes assumed a militant phase. " I am," he said once, " but little of a Unitarian, have little sympathy with the system of Priestley and Belsham, and stand aloof from all but those who strive and pray for clearer light."

In these words we get the key to his high character. He was a man who stood aside from none who were striving like himself to reach the light. In literature and philosophy this habit of mind elevated him to the rank of one of the best judicial critics of his day. In politics it gave him the authority that is necessarily wielded by a man of chivalrous aims, practical sagacity, serene temper, and reasonable mind. Born in Rhode Island, he spent his youth and manhood in Boston, and left upon that famous city the impress of an influence which has done much to make it the centre of culture and enlightenment in the Republic. It was Coleridge who said of him " he has the love of wisdom and the wisdom of love." To that singularly beautiful union in his nature may be traced the secret of his power. With him the " enthusiasm of humanity " was no mere phrase. It was a vivid, actuating motive of both conduct and thought. He did not love his fellow men as a matter of duty, but rather from natural inclination, inborn instinct, and deep conviction that the meanest of his kind was, in a sense, the image, however faded or distorted, of the Divine idea. We can fancy he would have felt as few save the purest and loftiest natures feel the profound significance of the mystic aphorism of Novalis : "We touch heaven when we lay our hand in a human grasp." To this sentiment we may attribute what gave rise to much painful controversy in his day, Dr. Channing's vigorous anti-slavery crusades, not to mention movements about which there was less difference of opinion, such as his untiring efforts to heighten the ambitions of the working class, to beautify and dignify the lot of labour, to bridge and not to deepen the gulf between the upper and the lower ranks in society, and to persuade liberty-loving men both in England and America that they had one great interest in common— the progress of their race—and ought to join hands like brothers working in amity for the advancement of that cause. No lasting good, he thought, could come to the world by any winking at wrongdoing, even though its victims might not, in the literal sense, suffer physical misery. If they were oppressed they must be delivered at all cost and hazard, else it would be the worse for the world that slothfully tolerated the injustice. Why, then, with such principles, it was asked, did Dr. Channing not aid the early advocates of Abolition with his potent influence—why did he hang back when they began to assail the "domestic institution" of the Southern States? The injustice done to Channing by impatient and hot-headed partisans has now been forgotten ; but, in explanation of his position in the great movement of which he ultimately became the intellectual head, we may say that it always had to be made very clear to Channing that there was an injustice to remedy, and that in remedying it justice would be done to all, and not to the few or the many, ere he would take up a cause and stand forward as its champion. He was pre-eminently a cautious, thoughtful, scholarly man, and he had difficulty in associating in his mind right principle with a cause that was advocated on wrong principles; in fact, it was to him impossible to conceive that any benefit could co-exist with an agitation whose leaders were provoking a death-struggle between rich and poor. "No good," he writes in one of his letters, "can come but from the spread of intellectual and moral power among all classes, and the union of all by a spirit of brotherhood. This moral renovation is itself the supreme good, and brings all others in its train."

Fortunately for the party of Abolition, Dr. Channing was in 1830 obliged to spend a winter in Santa Cruz, and there he came into direct contact with the institution the foundations of which he was destined to shake, and against which William Lloyd Garrison was, as a journeyman printer, and at the cost of his daily earnings, beginning to wage an uncompromising war. Channing saw that Slavery was in the most literal sense a soul-destroying institution; and that, alike in the slave and his owner, it created a combination of what he called "anti-social and sensual vices" that he could not but regard with horror and disgust. It was his mission to force this conviction on the intellectual and cultured class in the United States, and it was because he did his work with rare tact and excellent good sense that he enlisted in the party of Abolition nearly all the leaders of thought in the Great Republic. But when he was not toiling for his own country, as he said once himself, his thoughts turned to England. "Her energies and means of progress, her difficulties and distractions," he writes, in a letter to his friend, Mr. William Rathbone, "cannot but give rise to alternate hope and fear in one who loves her as much as I do." At that time our country had passed through the great reform struggle, and men of earnest natures were turning their attention to the social wants of the nation. Dr. Channing's sympathies went forth to meet those whom he recognized as co-workers with himself in the cause of human progress. It would be hard to overstate how much the party of social reform in this country was indebted to Channing's wise counsel and encouraging exhortations. He was a most voluminous letter-writer, and in his correspondence with English politicians of the philanthropic school, he was ever eager to push them into what he believed to be the right groove of agitation. "The fearful blot in your society," he wrote to one of his English friends, "is the degradation of your lower classes," and all our reforms, he was constantly arguing, were as nothing in the absence of anything like an effectual system of National Education. Then he was ever persuading his English friends to do what he did in America—press it on statesmen, as a political axiom, that war between two countries with such useful energies and rich resources should be regarded as an impossibility, "as too insane to be thought of," and that all difficulties between them must be settled peacefully. For his English friends, who used to tell him of the political dangers and difficulties they had to face, he always had an unvarying reply. Hope, patience, and faith in the right-heartedness of theEnglish people were, according to him, the feelings that public men should cherish, for if they were only true tothemselves all their perplexities would disappear. Dr. Channing, in fact, represented what was forty years ago a rare but most precious political influence in America—that of a clear and wise thinker who could not bring himself to regard England as a "foreign country," and to whom the very thought of any rivalry between the two nations save that of peaceful industry was unspeakably monstrous. On this, the morning of his centenary, Englishmen should therefore deem it a high privilege to pay a becoming tribute of respect to his memory. His name is not, perhaps, so familiar to the rising generation as it was to the great leaders of English thought and opinion into whose legacy of achievement and culture the present day has entered. Still, it is with pride that we recall the close connection which existed between them and the illustrious American who, after a long and noble life of intellectual toil, eight-and-thirty years ago passed away to his rest with this significant whisper on his lips, "I have received many messages from the Spirit."

Daily News, April 8th, 1880.

The meeting at St. James's Hall last night to celebrate the centenary of the birth of Dr. Channing was wisely not limited to those who share his religious views. The founder of New England Unitarianism, like his predecessor and sometime contemporary, Dr. Priestley, was too large and wide a man for his best influence to be limited to any religious sect. He may, perhaps, be longest remembered as the great preacher of doctrines then regarded as new and striking; but his place in the history of the United States is in some degree independent of his position in the history of opinion. The writings on which his theological reputation rests have perhaps, a wider fame, and certainly a far larger audience, than his more purely literary efforts ; but it was by his moral and social influence that he did most for his country. Dr. Channing was one of the makers of New England. He it was, more perhaps than any other man, who widened and transformed its narrow and provincial life. He found it colonial and left it national. He not only made Boston the centre of the religious views of which he was the most eloquent exponent, but helped to make it the intellectual capital of the United States. The War of Independence was brought to an end while he was still a child, and he went as a youth of fourteen to Harvard while Washington was in the second term of his Presidency. Neither the troubles nor the successes of the future Republic had then begun. When Channing went to Boston as a young preacher, in 1803, the opinion of the chief politicians of the young nation was that slavery would die out in the air of freedom. The States of Tennessee, Kentucky, and Vermont had just been added to the Union; and in that very year the country beyond the Mississippi had been added to the territories of the Republic by purchase from France. It was a time of intense mental activity in the newly liberated States. There was a reaction from political anxieties, which seemed to have been set at rest, towards social and theological problems. We may pass over the religious controversies which then raged in New England, though they claim a passing notice because it was as one of the founders of "the Boston religion," as it was called, that Channing was first known to fame. It was in somewhat later years, after these controversies had settled down, and the Federal Street Church was regarded with pride by men who did not share the religious views inculcated from its pulpit, that Channing's larger influence began. His celebrated Review of the Correspondence between President Adams and some supposed opponents of the Federal Union in Massachusetts was published in 1829. It was an eloquent and exhaustive statement of the reasons why the Union should be cherished as the guarantee and the guardian of American freedom. In this striking essay he foreshadowed in some degree, and probably did much to foster and increase that devotion to the Union which, thirty years after his death, took up the Southern challenge and destroyed slavery to save the Federal Government from dissolution.

It was not foreseen in Channing's early days that either the Union on the one hand, or slavery on the other, would become objects of passionate attachment. Channing's own chief political service to his country arose out of the aggressiveness of slavery, rather than from any aggressive attitude on his part towards slavery. He regarded his chief work as lying outside politics, and though he held and taught anti-slavery doctrines, he did not join the early anti-slavery movement. What Miss Martineau calls the Martyr Age of American Freedom does not form part of Channing's life. His doctrine of the dignity of human nature was inconsistent with all slavery, but he was content at first to leave its practical application to that particular evil to the gradual operation of the public sense of right and justice. But slavery soon found that it must have room, or die. The early founders of the Republic had been justified in their belief that it would not hold its own in a free State; but they did not know that new lands would open out on all sides over which it might spread. Channing, like many other men of quiet and gentle nature, held aloof from the early denouncers of what Garrison called "the covenant with hell." He seems to have hoped that the South would be more likely to abolish it if they were reasoned with, than if they were denounced. He proved to be wrong, or circumstances disappointed his expectation. But when the slave-owners overflowed into Mexican territory, and it was proposed to steal Texas from that neighbouring Republic in order to add another Slave State to the Union, Channing wrote to Mr. Clay a protest against the proposed act of national dishonesty which postponed, though it could not prevent, the crime. He was dead when the annexation was at last accomplished, but his protests against the threatened war, and the almost prophetic tone of his warning, had already done much to rouse the conscience of the nation. This, indeed, was Channing's great political service to his own, and the immediately following times. He made the people feel that a nation could not do injustice without suffering for it ; and that the petty cowardice of bullying weak neighbours was utterly unworthy of a free and self-respecting people. If he was late in publicly joining the Anti-Slavery protest, he at least gave it efficient and noble help when at last he was induced to speak; and he planted in the minds of the people of New England a sense of national responsibility for the wrong-doings of the Government, which had much to do with the great national uprising he did not live to see.

Probably some disappointment is now felt by many who come to Channing's writings for the first time, at the absence of anything which at once strikes them as original. It is difficult to realize that political and social views which are now the common possession of mankind can ever have had the charm of novelty. Nor indeed was there anything altogether new in Channing's doctrine of the dignity of man as man. It was new to the age to which he taught it; and it was received with so much enthusiasm because the time for it was ripe. It is the appropriate thought of a democratic age. It was Channing's merit, moreover, that he applied it not only to great political questions like that of slavery, but to social difficulties. In the America and in the England of that day it had scarcely yet occurred to reformers to begin with the habits and homes of the people themselves. The attempts at social reform took the shape of socialistic dreams, such as those which fascinated Hawthorne, and had charmed Channing himself in his earlier days. But it was his great service to give these efforts a severely practical shape. He urged the improvement of the outward circumstances in which the people lived, the bettering of their general condition, and the cleansing and brightening of their homes, as a direct object of philanthropic effort. The educational and sanitary movements which characterize the present century had scarcely begun even in the United States in Channing's boyhood; and they owe much of their impetus on both sides of the Atlantic to his teaching. We may say, indeed, that in his political and social writings, there is still much that the Americans especially need to learn. In the essay on the Union, of which we have already spoken, he not only vindicates Republican Government, but Free Trade. The essay was written in 1829, and anticipated therefore by many years the adoption of Free Trade principles in this country. Even at that early date he tells his countrymen not only that "every custom-house should be shut from Maine to Louisiana," which is one of his arguments for the Union, but that "the interests of human labour require that every fetter should be broken from the intercourse of nations, that the most distant nations should exchange all their products, whether of manual or of intellectual labour, as freely as the members of the same community." This is only one illustration of the clearness of his intellectual vision. In this matter he is still far before the great bulk of his countrymen; and it would be a happy circumstance if the new attention called by this centenary celebration to his writings should induce his own countrymen to learn from the teacher of whom they have such just reason to be proud how, in his own words, "Happy it would be for us could tariffs be done away with, for with them would be abolished fruitful causes of national jealousies, of war, of perjury, of smuggling, of innumerable frauds and crimes, and of harassing restraint on that commerce which should be free as the winds."

Anti-Slavery Reporter, May 1st, 1880.

ON April 7th a very large assembly met in St. James's Hall, London, to celebrate the hundredth anniversary of the birth of William Ellery Channing. The invitation freely extended to some of the foremost representatives of other Churches, and the wise and catholic selection of speakers, showed that Channing was rightly regarded as too great to be confined within the walls of any particular sect, and that his own lessons of catholic wisdom had sunk into the hearts of those who claim him as one of their foremost leaders in the cause of religious freedom and progress. The bond of union which held together the vast assembly was common veneration for the saintly goodness which is the heart and essence of the Gospel, and the perception of the great principle, which was the real inspiration of Channing's life and teaching, that religious communion is altogether independent of intellectual differences of opinion.

The Methodist, April 16th, 1880.

THE Channing Centenary was celebrated on Wednesday last. A large and enthusiastic meeting was held in St. James's Hall. We were much interested in the principal features of the gathering. Dr. Martineau was the first speaker. He gave a sketch of Channing which was biographical, historical, critical, and philosophical. We never heard anything more perfect. It was given with exquisite ease. Its spiritual qualities were equal to its literary finish. The Doctor had brief notes in his hand, but he made very little use of them. His tone and expression are exceedingly devotional — almost ecclesiastical. He is the representative of a great deal more than a merely intellectual type of Christianity. Baldwin Brown followed with a paper on Channing as a spiritual teacher. He had a splendid reception, and he raised the audience to a pitch of excitement. He attacked the old Calvinistic theology, and said that it was inevitable that Unitarianism should rise as a protest against it. He then lifted his face from his manuscript, and said, "You will not agree with what I am going to say next, but I suppose some free speech is allowed here." He secured a tremendous cheer, and then he said, "Here the function of Unitarianism ends." This opinion was received with a good-natured laugh, but it was evidently not accepted. Thomas Hughes read a paper on Channing's work in opposition to slavery. The paper was full of the genial characteristics of its author, but the evening was advanced; the audience began to disperse, so the effect of the paper was partly lost. Dr. Martineau then read a short paper by the Dean of Westminster, the object of which seemed to be to show how near Channing's standpoint was to that of Broad Churchmen. Several brief speeches followed. The whole audience was evidently under the influence of what I may call the Channing spirit.

The Christian Globe, April 15th, 1880.

WILLIAM ELLERY CHANNING, whose centenary was celebrated last week on both sides of the Atlantic with becoming enthusiasm, has been well and truly called "a great and good man." Not among Anglo-Saxon speaking races alone, but among all civilized and liberty-loving people, his memory will be cherished with affectionate esteem. For he was in every sense of the word a "benefactor" of his fellow-men. Putting aside his great intellectual claims as a writer, and the fact that he was a leader of thought when "light and leading" were sorely needed both in England and America, he was pre-eminently and above all things a lover of mankind. He it was who shaped into action the beautiful and noble thought of Universal Brotherhood, which became the polar star of the lives of a noble host of social reformers, like Elihu Burritt. Coleridge was so impressed with his writings, his character, and his work, that he said of him, "he has the love of wisdom and the wisdom of love." There is a singular charm about everything he has written, an indescribable something which fascinates the reader, and yet the ideas do not strike one as being altogether new. They are rather like the sounds of some forgotten but once familiar strain. His sentences are not simply exquisitely moulded, but there is in them an inexpressible depth of human pathos. They remind one of the grand old saying, "I am a man, and everything that interests mankind interests me." The noble part he took in the "Slavery Abolition" and the temperance movement is well-known to the world at large. And though his sense of justice and rectitude induced some of the more impetuous opponents of the baneful "domestic institution" to suspect him of luke-warmness and "halting betwixt two opinions," their misgivings and doubts were soon scattered to the winds when he became their intellectual leader in the fight. It was not a sense of fear, but an innate love of right, which for a brief season withheld the arm that was afterwards upraised. His heart was in the right, and he never turned a deaf ear to conscience. But he was too thoughtful, too circumspect and wise to become a blind leader of the blind. In other words, he saw that the conflict was inevitable—that the struggle must come sooner or later, that slavery must cease to be; but he would not lend himself to a "leap in the dark." His motives for this hesitancy were at first misinterpreted, but time and the magnificent service he afterwards rendered to the cause have made it all clear. Many eminent men, clerical and lay, were present at the celebration which took place in St. James's Hall, including the Rev. Baldwin Brown, Dr. Carpenter, the Rev. Dr. Martineau, the Rev. Professor Plumptre, and others well-known to fame.) ean Stanley, who was unable to be present, paid an eloquent tribute to the worth of Dr. Channing in a paper which was read to the assembly by Dr. Martineau. The learned Dean drew special attention to the wide appreciation of his genius and the catholicity of his religious sentiments. In support of this view he quoted Channing's own words as the most effectual answer to the charge which his enemies so often used against him—"I am but little of a Unitarian, have little sympathy with the system of Priestly or of Belsham, and stand aloof from all but those who strive and pray for clearer light." That was the secret of his power, of his wonderful influence, the heartfelt never-ceasing yearning for "light, more light," which was put into words, that will ever live, by Matthew

Arnold. In the opinion of the Dean, Channing contributed in no mean degree towards the right appreciation of, and fixing the attention of Christendom on, the truly divine ; the truly permanent, supernatural elements of Christianity—moral and spiritual. In fact, he stood in the highest ranks of Christian men. The Rev. Baldwin Brown bore similar testimony to his character and genius. His interpretation of Channing's belief was that if religion was meant for man in all times, then it must necessarily include the whole field of his legitimate interests. There was no human interest which he did not connect with the gospel ; and, to sum up his virtues, he was the most eloquent philanthropist of his age— an assertion which will certainly not be disputed by any one who is familiar with the stirring and touching strains in which he pleaded for the rights of humanity at large. Like Welsey, he was cosmopolitan in feeling and sentiment, and the world was "his parish." He viewed with as much dismay as Charles Kingsley did, and as some of the noblest humanitarians of our own day do, the unbridged gulf that separated then, as now, the lowest from the so-called highest classes. He regarded the degradation of the lower classes as "the most fearful blot" on English society. And in one of his letters he said— " No good can ever come but from the spread of intellectual and moral power among all classes, and the union of all by a spirit of brotherhood. This moral renovation is itself the supreme good, and brings all others in its train." Such was the man whose memory has been so deservedly honoured, and whose name will live on the imperishable bead-roll of the world's great men.

The Inquirer, April 3, 1880.

CHANNING'S function, as John James Tayler—himself a man of kindred genius—wrote long ago in his "Retrospect of the Religious Life of England," was rather that of the prophet than that of the scholar and philosopher. His scattered pieces have gone out into the world like so many oracles of ancient wisdom. He uttered forth, in tones of such deep conviction and thrilling persuasiveness, sentiments and aspirations which lie folded up in every human breast, that he has called out a wide responsive sympathy, and made thousands receive, through the kindling medium of his affectionate spirit, a fresh communication of religious life.

This is the real secret of the influence which Channing exerts, and will continue to exert, when critical inquirers have done their work, and philosophical systems are succeeded by new theories, which are often only ancient speculations dressed in new guise. The influence of the prophet is always greater than that of the scholar or the philosopher, because he appeals to the permanent instincts and aspirations which are the same in all ages, and are never superseded by any possible discoveries of the latest science, or the ingenious speculations of the most advanced thought.

It is the glory of Channing that he proclaimed with a breadth of view and sweetness of love the Gospel of the "enthusiasm of humanity," as he learned it from the simple teachings of Christ, unalloyed by the traditions and accretions of ages. In an age which was rapidly outgrowing old forms of thought, and groping with somewhat vague ideas and halting steps towards the new and unknown, it was the rare distinction of Channing that he combined reverence for all that was worthy of reverence in the past, with an unwavering allegiance to the new law of progress, and a steadfast devotion to the principle of freedom which recognized no limitations, and was not dismayed even by the strange and wild vagaries of its more enthusiastic disciples.

Channing is often characterized by some among ourselves as an advocate of *conservative* Unitarianism as opposed to the more progressive and advanced aspects of that faith. We are unwilling to claim Channing as a partisan of any school of thought among us, and his aspirations were far too catholic to be "cabined, cribbed, confined" within any of our mere sectarian or sectional systems. But such a representation of him as that to which we have referred does marked injustice to the wide catholicity and unbounded faith in freedom and progress, which were far more characteristic of him than belief in any particular set of dogmas or mere opinions. It is true that he retained through life a firm grasp of historical Christianity as the Divine power which ensures the real moral and spiritual progress of the world; but who among us is not ready to believe the same, if only we distinguish between the permanent essence of Christianity and its transitory and fleeting envelopments? It is true, also, that he entertained through life a more or less unwavering faith in the supernaturalism of the Gospels, mainly on the ground of the difficulty of separating the miracles from the moral and religious teachings with which they seem inextricably interwoven. But on all these subjects Channing's mind was open as the day to new truth, always aspiring for "more light;" and he was one of the last to regard with the old conservative suspicion or distrust the critical inquiries of those of his brethren who believed less than himself, or seemed in their distinctive criticism to be destroying much that he deeply valued, so long as they retained the faith in truth and reverence for goodness which he believed to be the heart of the Gospel.

The Unitarian Herald, April 16th, 1880.

CHANNING was, supremely, a reconciling soul; and it is now the highest mark of his power that in the celebrations of his centenary the lines of sectarianism disappear amidst the communion of souls who have been touched by his spirit and renewed by the breath of his power. Unitarian he was, and those who now wish to claim him as almost if not altogether orthodox, must surely forget that his American contemporaries were not sparing in their condemnation of his theology; and they must also forget that their claim of Channing's nearness to the Evangelicism of to-day arises from no approximation to orthodoxy on his part, but from the gradual approach of orthodoxy to liberal religion. Still, we have no desire to emphasize Channing's Unitarianism. The secret of his living and still growing power is in that subtle and undefinable thing which we call his spirit— a mirror in which those who come near him see the best and purest in themselves. Channing is not the less but the more spiritual that he fed his soul with those universal truths of religion which are as old as the first man's vague aspirations, as fresh as the trust of the new-born child, as permanent as the crying out of the heart for the living God. It is this which unites to him, and makes one in his presence, men who by their theologies are divided and stand apart. It is the spirit that is identical beneath all forms, and that resolves noble souls into the harmony of man. Channing wins and reigns by virtue of the religious sentiment; and embodied as it was in him it proves what Emerson says of it: "Wonderful is its power to charm and to command. It makes man illimitable."

The centenary meetings have been witnesses to the admiration and gratitude which men of all schools of theology pay to the memory of Dr. Channing as the eloquent exponent—nay, as the incarnation in a saintly life of doing good, of the permanent and inexhaustible simplicities of religion.

． ． ． ． ． ． ．

Channing is one of the true race of prophets, to whom

men are drawn by the eternal revelation which is in their hearts, and which ever goes forth anew to take possession of the world. A *fresh* testimony, we say, and yet one scarcely needed, for as Mr. C. T. Brooks, in his pleasant and graphic sketch, " Channing : a Centennial Memory," just to hand, abundantly shows, the name and memory of Channing have received a cordial, Christian, and human recognition beyond the bounds of his own and any sect or land.

The Christian Life, April 10th, 1880.

THE world offers its admiring homage to the memory of the Unitarian saint and philanthropist. No tribute more impressive has ever, in the modern history of Christendom, been rendered to any leader of the religious thoughts of men. For Channing was not only a heretic, but a heretic of the kind least favoured by the conforming throng. He was an outspoken heretic ; a heretic who boldly took and proudly wore a denominational title, the very sound of which is an offence to the timid, an alarm to the orthodox, a reproach to the indifferent. Channing was a Unitarian, and whoever reads Channing must confess, in spite of prejudice, and in the teeth of prepossession, that to a Unitarian may belong not only the fervent glow of moral enthusiasm, the unquenchable instinct of religious and social freedom, and the lively zeal of human progress and development, but other qualities also, not usually associated in popular estimation with the Unitarian name. For Channing stands before the eyes of mankind a witness for spirituality of the highest order, for Christianity of the clearest and most unmistakable kind, for the real presence of the kingdom of Christ on earth. These are attributes which the Churches are slow to recognise in union with overt heresy. Yet precisely in these, by common consent, does Channing rise conspicuous above the multitude of Christ's followers, whatever be their type of faith, whatever their ecclesiastical connection.

Many a holy man has won the united love of Christendom in virtue of philanthropic energies and evangelical zeal, and often these have thrown his special ecclesiastical position completely into the shade. We forget that Oberlin was a Lutheran, Zschokke a Zwinglian, in the absorbing interest of their services to the common weal, and the gospel of practical piety and righteousness. But Channing figured so prominently as the vindicator of a strongly marked theology, he identified himself so heroically with the cause of that Church which he adorned and upheld, that he can never be treated as other than a Unitarian. The preacher of the Baltimore sermon, the author of the *Moral Argument against Calvinism*, is separated by an impassable line from the men of mere religious latitude, who belong to every Church and none.

It is distinctively as a Unitarian, as the pioneer of that pure and free, yet firm and Christian theology, which is the hope of the nations still sunk in superstition and error, that Italy and Sweden, France and Iceland, avow by the mouths of their noblest sons their acceptance of the leadership of Channing. The great American is their religious emancipator, and their theological guide. His writings are the handbook of their spiritual ideas.

All the more honour to those who, not identifying themselves with the distinctly affirmed doctrinal position of Channing, cannot withhold their generous admiration of the man, the philanthropist, and the Christian. When candid Wesley said of Thomas Firmin that he had long held, as a matter of course, that no denier of the doctrine of the Trinity could be truly pious, but that facts had changed his view, he altered the whole aspect of the question at issue between orthodoxy and heterodoxy. Firmin is a merely local name. But the character of Channing is the common treasure of Christian minds. His influence is world-wide. It is not too much to say that Channing has for ever lifted the Unitarian controversy out of its old position as a conflict between Christian and heretic, and compelled it to be seen in its true light, as a generous rivalry, on equal terms, between divergent types of the common Christian belief and spirit.

We cannot over-estimate, and find it hard sufficiently to express our debt, as a Christian community, to this best and greatest among our great and good. But if his spirit could find a voice amid the joys and triumphs of this our glad commemoration of his birth, it would counsel us to-day, in his own sweet persuasive way, not to waste this occasion in mere jubilation and satisfied reverie, but to be up and doing for the cause to which he consecrated himself with such rich power and such rare gentleness. The Channing Centennial is a solemn call to each and all the lovers of Channing to make the next hundred years full of living evidences of our devotion to the glorious truths which claimed him as their convincing exponent. If, as faithful servants of Channing's Lord, we gird our energies to this sacred duty, the happy hours of our thankful celebration will not have been spent in vain.

Woodfall and Kinder, Printers, Milford Lane, Strand, London, W.C.

www.ingramcontent.com/pod-product-compliance
Lightning Source LLC
Chambersburg PA
CBHW021353230426
43666CB00006B/509